Korean
Gardens

Korean Gardens

Tradition, Symbolism and Resilience

Jill Matthews

Carlsbad, CA and Seoul

Korean Gardens: Tradition, Symbolism and Resilience

Edited by Hahm Minji
Designed by Lee Hyehee, Jung Deunhae

First published in 2018
Third printing, 2022
by Hollym International Corp., Carlsbad, CA, USA
Phone 760 814 9880
http://www.hollym.com   **e-Mail** contact@hollym.com

⎰⎱ Hollym

Published simultaneously in Korea
by Hollym Corp., Publishers, Seoul, Korea
Phone +82 2 734 5087   **Fax** +82 2 730 5149
http://www.hollym.co.kr   **e-Mail** hollym@hollym.co.kr

ISBN: 978-1-56591-490-2
Library of Congress Control Number: 2018940390

Printed in Korea

This book is dedicated to the cultural resilience and tenacity of the Korean people as expressed in their unique and beautiful gardening tradition.

Western Gardeners' Guide
to the Essence of Korean Traditional Gardens

Korean gardens are unique, and have a history that goes back over two millennia. They are not grand and ostentatious like some of the Renaissance gardens of Europe. They do not seek to dominate and re-shape their natural surroundings or create awe in the beholder. They are not expressions of man's triumph over nature. Rather Korean gardens strive to be in harmony with nature and to encourage the quiet contemplation of the natural world and are altogether more humble in their conception.

Despite their distinctive qualities, Korean gardens are often incorrectly assumed to be mere variants of Chinese or Japanese gardening traditions. Korea's gardens deserve to be more widely appreciated as a separate and venerable gardening tradition, and I hope that this book will help them to be better appreciated in the English-speaking world.

I am a qualified Horticulturist and Landscape Designer trained in Australia. I have travelled widely in Asia for many years. Over the last 30 years I have made repeated visits to Korea and have become an admirer of many aspects of Korean culture, particularly the gardens both traditional and modern. Unfortunately I do not speak or read Korean or Chinese. Therefore in addition to my own observations, I can only rely upon books and other resources about Korean gardens if they are written in English. There are few of these and I have drawn from them extensively to write this book. I owe a particular debt to Professor Min Kyung-hyun's wonderful book *Korean Gardens*; Professor Heo Kyun's profound *Gardens of Korea—Harmony with Intellect and Nature*; and the more recent *Korean Traditional Landscape* written by thirteen Professors of landscape architecture and related fields, published by the Korean Institute of Traditional Architecture. Details of these books and others on which I have relied are in Further Readings. From each of these books I have absorbed many ideas and have occasionally quoted directly from them. In a sense this book is also theirs and I thank them all for their extensive contributions to it.

Numerous gardens in South Korea are open to the public and I have enjoyed visiting many of them over the years. Unlike the lovely Japanese gardens of Kyoto or the great classical Chinese gardens of Suzhou, Korean gardens are not clustered together in easily visited areas. Because of the importance of appropriate site selection and Korea's unique and violent history, surviving solitary Korean gardens are often found in isolated and out of the way places which require some effort to reach. To encourage readers to visit I have tried to provide practical location information for each garden I describe. I find that the more you know about Korean gardens, the more you see and understand when you visit them. I wrote this book for enthusiastic amateur gardeners more familiar with western or other more widely known Asian gardening traditions. I invite you to use it to find out where Korean gardens are, how to visit them and, above all, to understand the significance of the plants, structures and symbolism you will find in them when you do. I am sure you will come to be as enthusiastic and admiring of Korean gardens as I am.

Acknowledgments

I wish to give particular thanks to Mr. An Sin-young, Director of the Korean Culture Centre in Sydney, who has encouraged me greatly in the writing of this book and gave crucial help by obtaining the agreement of other Korean government institutions to my use of their photographs. I owe an additional debt to his wife, Mrs. Lee Se-jung, who gave great assistance by locating Internet resources only available in Korean. Ms. Kim So-young of the Korean Culture Centre did much to assist me to contact various potential publishers in Korea. Brother Anthony (An Son-jae), President of the Royal Asiatic Society Korea Branch was an early supporter of this project, as were the late Peter Bartholomew, another long-time resident and friend of Korea and Professor Sung Jong-sang the Dean of the Graduate School of Environmental Studies, Seoul National University and Gil Teague of Florilegium books in Sydney. The late Professor Suh Chung-sok of the Korea Research Institute at the University of New South Wales and my friend the late Ben Johnston both took the trouble to write several references in support of grant applications to assist my field research, as did my friend Sylvia Midgett former President of the Hong Kong Gardening Society, although alas, all to no avail. My good friend Professor Park Whon-il procured for me as a gift a very rare, useful and out-of-print book on Korean Gardens, did much to help organise my field trips to rural gardens and made numerous suggestions which greatly improved the manuscript.

Thanks and acknowledgment are due to the following Korean institutions for use of photographs: the Korean Tourism Organization (KTO), especially Ms. Jade Park Min-jung, Deputy Director of their Sydney office; the Korean National Arboretum (KNA), especially Dr. Jin Hye-young the author of two KNA books, one on Joseon traditional gardens and one on Buddhist temple gardens; and the Korean Cultural Heritage Administration.

Mr. Eric Oey, CEO of Tuttle Books in Singapore gave much sensible advice about the basic structure of the book.

I was very lucky to have the excellent and enthusiastic Ms. Ha Soon-young as my Editor at Hollym. She shares my passion for Korean gardens and did much to enhance the presentation of the whole book.

Although ultimate responsibility for the content remains with me, several people have read some or all of the manuscript and offered many helpful suggestions. Professor Park Whon-il was an early and meticulous reader. Mr. An Sin-young and my good friend Stuart Read, Australian cultural landscape specialist, both spent many hours they could ill spare, reading and checking practical details. Professor Jeong Sang-jo of Seoul National University, Ms. Kim Kyung-hee of ICOMOS (International Council on Monuments and Sites) and David Kendal all clarified issues I could not.

None have been so assiduous as my beloved husband Graham Greenleaf who has steadfastly believed in this book every step of the way, even accompanying me on arduous field trips, sleeping on the floors of *hanok* with ceilings too low for his Western frame, asking only for a bowl of *makgeolli* and a good Korean meal at the end of long days on the road. He stopped me giving up on this project times and I cannot thank him enough.

Jill Matthews
jill@austlii.edu.au

Contents

Part 3. Tables and Diagrams

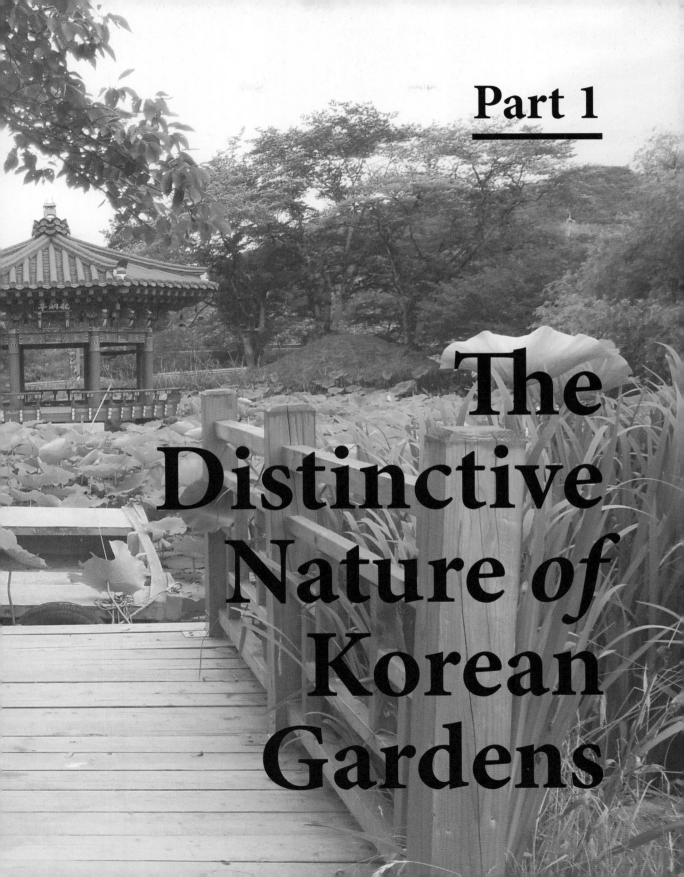

Part 1

The Distinctive Nature of Korean Gardens

01   A Brief History of Korean Gardens: Cultural Resilience

Koreans have been making distinctive and beautiful gardens for at least 2000 years and continue to do so. The profession of landscape designer was well established in Korea before a Japanese princess commissioned a Korean to design the first royal pleasure garden recorded in Japan. Few gardens in Europe, not even the earliest scientific botanic gardens in Padua and Florence, are as old as the earliest surviving gardens in Korea. Several centuries before the great landed estates in England were installing their manure powered pineapple pits and competing with each other to produce the finest hothouse-grown pineapples, Korean horticulturists had invented a form of insulated, heated, rice-straw-walled greenhouse. In these they could force plum trees to blossom in mid-winter. This was no mean achievement, despite the reaction of the conservative Joseon monarch to whom the first forced branch of blossom was presented, who remarked that he would have preferred to have seen the blossom in its correct season.

No matter how many times foreign invaders or civil wars destroy them, Koreans rebuild their gardens. The Korean peninsula is unfortunately situated between mainland China and the Japanese archipelago. An unavoidable consequence of this geographical fact has been constant invasion from both directions since prehistoric times. Sometimes these invasions have been relatively benign and merely involved dynastic marriages, and the peaceful adoption by the Korean elite of foreign ideas such as Chinese myth, script, literature, and the philosophies of Daoism, Buddhism and Confucianism. (This was particularly so during the Silla period when many Koreans studied abroad in Tang dynasty in China.) However more often they have been violent and involved the deliberate destruction of Korean cultural heritage, including gardens. In historic times there were major violent invasions of peninsula by the Chinese Han starting in 109 BC and there was a very damaging series of invasions by the Mongols between AD 1231 and AD 1270. However, by far the most destructive invasions have been by the Japanese. The invasions in by General Toyotomi Hideyoshi (the Imjin Wars) between 1592 and 1598 involved the deliberate burning down of almost every wooden building in Korea, palaces, temples and garden pavilions included. It is almost impossible to visit an old garden in Korea today where the signage does not state that it was partially or fully destroyed during these invasions. This tradition of vandalism and attempted cultural genocide by the Japanese continued during their occupation of modern Korea between 1910 and 1945 and is described more fully in Chapter 6 (Chinese and Japanese Influences).

Between 1950 and 1953 the Korean War was fought between North Korea and its ally China, and South Korea, supported by the United States and numerous allies, under the UN flag. This most recent war involved major, although less targeted, destruction. It left Korea divided in two and

South Korea so devastated and impoverished that its remaining resources needed to be directed to the immediate survival needs of the population and could not be spared for the restoration or maintenance of even the oldest and most valued gardens until relatively recently. However the Koreans are an extremely resilient people. Their economic recovery had been fast and sustained and in recent decades has enabled the South Korean government to begin once again to restore and reconstruct many of its important gardens such as those surrounding the royal palaces in Seoul. In addition the families and descendants of the original garden-makers have once again assumed responsibility for the maintenance and, when necessary the reconstruction, of their ancestors' gardens. This current process of Korean garden restoration in the 21st century, particularly in Seoul, is a fine example of cultural resilience in the face of extreme adversity and continues a tradition of restoration and reconstruction that has existed for at least 2000 years.

Despite these repeated invasions and wars, a surprising number of gardens or fragments of gardens have survived, often for hundreds of years. Many of the earliest major gardens were created in what is now North Korea and cannot be visited by Westerners. It is uncertain how many of them have survived. In South Korea, the oldest remnant of a Korean pleasure garden, the Haeamjeong pavilion in Gangwondo province, was first built in 1361 and first rebuilt five hundred years ago in 1530. Gungnamji, a beautiful pond first built in AD 634 by the Baekje dynasty King Mu as part of his palace garden, still exists, although opinions differ about the accuracy of its restoration. Most of the surviving gardens in South Korea are of later dates, mainly from the Silla and Joseon periods, 57 BC ~ AD 935 and AD 1392 ~ 1910 respectively.

In newly prosperous South Korea, many surviving traditional gardens both private and public, are being refurbished. Koreans have been excellent and enthusiastic gardeners for many generations and today can once again afford to make new gardens for pleasure. The profession of Landscape Architect is a venerable and highly respected one, which is taught at University level. Contemporary Korean banknotes express Korean pride in this long horticultural tradition, several featuring famous Confucian scholar-gardeners and their gardens. The ongoing 'Greening of Seoul' project, which includes the planting and transplanting of hundreds of thousands of street trees, major new landscaping of urban green space and civic subsidies for the creation of numerous and sustainable roof gardens in the city, is testament to this. It is an astonishing example of cultural continuity to see how many of these modern gardens, and how much of this recent landscaping, refer to the old gardening styles and symbols.

02 What Makes Korean Gardens Distinctive?

At least nine typical features of Korean gardens combine to create their distinctive character: use of natural topography; site selection; lack of boundaries; borrowed landscape; syncretic symbolism; plant selection and cultivation; proportion of buildings to garden; constant rebuilding; and public accessibility.

Use of Natural Topography

One profound effect of the layers of spiritual and religious belief embedded in the Korean psyche is a deeply held reverence for nature and a marked reluctance to disturb it unnecessarily. Korean gardens are never built on the top of mountains so as to dominate the natural world below. Rather they are sited to nestle into the existing natural topography with as little disturbance as possible. Although water is an important element in traditional Korean gardens it is never subdued and pumped uphill to feed fountains or ostentatious cascades. No rivers are diverted or canals built to water Korean gardens. At most the natural flow of rivers or streams may be slowed to create quiet reaches of reflective water or to reveal slightly rearranged local stones or rocks. The expensive and disruptive transportation of enormous trophy rocks from far away places, such as one sees in the intriguing Chinese gardens of Suzhou or the grand Boboli garden in Florence, is a concept very foreign to Korean garden construction. In fact major earth moving of any sort seems to have been frowned upon except where absolutely necessary to enable the erection of buildings or the creation of small symbolic ponds or the resiting of mature trees.

Korean gardens are not expressions of power or the capacity of man to subdue nature such as Versailles in France or the great renaissance gardens of Rome and Tuscany in Italy are. Korean gardens are not designed to miniaturize and replicate or improve on the natural world as the beautiful Japanese gardens of Kyoto are. They are not intended create havens from harsh external environment such as the great Islamic paradise gardens, built to make the heat of the plains of India or the waterless deserts of the Middle East tolerable. Rather, Korean gardens are intended to exist in harmony with Korea's climate and natural surroundings and to enhance the enjoyment of both in an unobtrusive, almost humble way.

Site Selection

The Korean principles of geomancy (*pungsu*) are explained more fully in chapter 3 (Spirituality and Korean Garden). They have pervaded site selection for palaces, temples and royal tombs and their associated gardens, for more than a thousand years. *Pungsu* was never, however, the justification for aggressive modification of landscapes, as is common in other gardening traditions. The aim was to achieve human developments, including gardens, which were in balance and harmony with their natural surroundings and which did the minimum disruption to the landscape. This emphasis on careful and appropriate site selection and environmentally friendly development could be seen as the foundation of Korean landscape design. It may in fact be one of the reasons why so many Korean gardens have survived for so long in comparison to say the gardens of the great Mogul emperors in India, which were so often abandoned and died once natural or man-made catastrophes disrupted their elaborate and expensive irrigation systems.

As part of the twenty-first century restorations of the major surviving gardens in South Korea, great attention is paid to the restoration of their original *pungsu* energy flows. A good example of this is the uncovering, de-polluting and landscaping of the Cheonggyecheon stream which not only enhances the amenity of downtown Seoul, but is also widely understood to assist in the restoration of the original *pungsu* energy flows surrounding the main royal palace Gyeongbokgung.

Whatever your views about the 'validity' of *pungsu*, it has clearly led to the selection of beautiful sites for all the old gardens considered in this book and even to their survival in hard times, and it undoubtedly remains a serious factor in contemporary Korean garden design and restoration. When visiting Korean gardens today do take note of the site selection, including the presence and direction of running water and protective hills, the positioning of copses of trees and pagodas and the use of borrowed landscape. All of these elements of the garden will have been informed by the principles of *pungsu*.

Lack of Boundaries

Joseon royal palace gardens, and Confucian academic institution gardens, are enclosed, often by very beautiful walls of rammed earth, tile and brick or stone, however, many Korean gardens are not enclosed and there is no obvious boundary between the garden and the surrounding borrowed landscape. The gardens surrounding Buddhist temples, royal tomb parks and scholarly retreat gardens are usually sited amidst forests, and the deliberate plantings of the gardens simply shade off into the surrounding natural wilderness. Indeed, as detailed later, the ritual walkways leading to Buddhist temples are deliberately constructed to encourage visitors to experience the pleasures of barely cultivated natural forest and untamed streams before they enter the more structured garden immediately surrounding the temples themselves.

Borrowed Landscape
While many gardening traditions claim to use borrowed landscape to

Meongokheon garden near Damyang is perfectly sited to 'borrow' the outline of the surrounding hills.
© KNA (Korea National Arboretum)

advantage, Korean garden designers must be world champions at the practice. The careful site selection dictated by geomantic theory leads to glorious backdrops for all but the most urban of Korean gardens. If you have the opportunity to visit the Silla dynasty tomb park in Gyeongju, observe how the shape of the tumuli tombs exactly echoes the outline of the distant enclosing hills, or should you happen to be at Haeinsa temple at dusk as the clouds roll theatrically down the encompassing mountains, you will know what I mean.

Syncretic Symbolism

As explained in the next chapter Korean spirituality is syncretic and contains elements of animism, Shamanism, Daoism, Buddhism and Confucianism. Symbols and influences from all of these can be seen in Korean gardens often together in the same garden.

Wind-sown hollyhock thriving against an old village wall on Bogildo Island.
© Jill Matthews

Plant Selection and Cultivation

The plants cultivated in Korean gardens and the mode of cultivation are both very influenced by the fundamental idea that gardens are to be in harmony with nature and to disrupt it as little as possible. Whereas the practice of bonsai is widespread in Japan, and the similar practice of *penzai* (or *penjing*) is widespread in China, Korean gardens do not emphasise miniaturization of plants. Some private aristocratic homes may have small collections of bonsai trees in pots. In the courtyards of Buddhist temples where fire is an ever-present threat, some trees may be pruned to keep them smaller (and even occasionally cloud-pruned for aesthetic effect) but even in these cases, the preference is to select naturally small trees, plant them directly in the ground and allow them to reach their full potential, rather than to deliberately stunt trees which would otherwise have grown to be much larger. In a similar vein, serendipitous flowers are encouraged. It is common to see wind-sown hollyhocks, cosmos or other daisies allowed to flourish to brighten walls or pathways in traditional Korean villages.

Pot culture of trees and plants is not common. Plants are more often selected to survive in the ground all year round rather than requiring cossetting under cover until they bloom. There is a clear preference for species plants, such as tough daisy-like chrysanthemums, which will re-emerge in

25

Korean gardeners prefer simple robust species such as this rose climbing on a wall in Hahoe village, rather than modern, fussy, overbred hybrids. © Jill Matthews

Part I. The Distinctive Nature of Korean Gardens

the same spot in the garden year after year. Spectacular large florist-style artificially selected cultivars of spider or mop head chrysanthemums with their requirements for staking, pruning and protection from the elements, are almost never seen in traditional Korean gardens. The same can be said for the varieties of iris, azalea, peony, daisy, rose and many other annuals and perennials grown outdoors in Korean gardens. It is hard to imagine Korean gardeners competing to grow the largest number of blooms on a single chrysanthemum plant and then exhibiting them briefly under cover in major public gardens every autumn in the way that Japanese gardeners do.

Plant selection is another point of difference. Because of the shared Chinese literary tradition, many of the trees, shrubs and plants which appear in Chinese gardens, art and literature are also cultivated in Korean gardens, however in addition many others of no particular literary or symbolic note are cultivated. The Korean plant palette is much less restricted than it is in other Asian gardens. Indigenous plants are encouraged in naturalised meadows, particularly in royal tomb and Buddhist temple gardens. Many plants are selected whose blooms, foliage and berries, emphasise the changing of the seasons. This is especially so in flower terraces, known as *hwagye*, which are common in almost all types of Korean gardens including domestic, royal palace and Buddhist temple. Here ebullient combinations of flowers of many colours and forms change with the seasons, perhaps a metaphor for the Daoist and Buddhist preoccupation with the cycle of life and the possibility of attaining brilliant enlightenment or immortality.

The types of trees cultivated in Korean gardens are also significant because so many of them are native to Korea. Trees such as the Chinese juniper (*Juniperus chinensis*), the Japanese elm (*Zelkova serrata*) and Japanese dogwood trees (*Cornus kousa*), received either their Latin or common names because they were first discovered by Europeans in China and Japan. However many trees have a much broader natural range than this. They are just three examples of trees, which are endemic to the Korean peninsula as well as to China and Japan and widely cultivated in traditional Korean gardens. It seems that Korean gardeners valued the virtues of native trees and vegetation, perfectly adapted as they are to local conditions, long before 20th century garden designers started promoting 'native' gardens as environmentally responsible and aesthetically pleasing alternatives to gardens filled with high maintenance exotics.

The particular reverence that Koreans demonstrate for trees is unique and probably dates back to sylvan prehistory and perhaps the Korean Dangun creation myth itself. Trees are only very rarely regimented into straight avenues and trimmed hedges are unknown. In South Korea there is a major reafforestation project underway which includes the planting of thousands of street trees in cities and the inclusion of many trees in the major traditional garden restoration projects now in train, particularly in Seoul. South Koreans regard the massive

Hostas, dog rose, Boston ivy, clover and evening primroses provide colour and interest year round in this *hwagye* at Haeinsa temple. © Jill Matthews

This ancient Dangsan Zelkova tree was old before Suwon fortress and palace was built around it. Despite its fragility, is still revered and frequently decked with fresh votive flags. © Jill Matthews

deforestation currently occurring in North Korea with horror. Often individual trees with special historic associations are not removed from gardens, even when they are senescent or have died. Traditional villages each had a special holy tree known as *dangsan*. Still today special ceremonies are performed around *dangsan* trees involving the tying of flags, the placing of offerings of food and the pouring of rice wine (*makgeolli*) and when the advance of modernity threatens them, huge expense and expertise is applied to relocate them safely.

Proportion of Buildings to Garden

Another distinguishing characteristic of Korean gardens is the proportion of

A series of garden pavilions such as this Chinese style one, dot the watercourse, each separated by swathes of woodland, in the Biwon garden within Changdeokgung palace. © KNA

buildings and "hard landscaping" compared to the proportion of plants and general greenery. In some Chinese gardens, the number of pavilions and the extent of the rock arrangements and dividing masonry walls is so great that there is little room for actual garden plants. This is not the case in Korean gardens where human structures and constructions sit unobtrusively amidst great areas of woodland, cultivated meadows and gardens.

Constant Rebuilding

The turbulent history of Korea has made this attribute of its gardens a necessity. It is almost never possible to say 'this garden is 500 years old,' but it is often possible to say 'there has been a garden here for 500 years; some of the trees in it are at least that old and the renovated garden structures adhere to the original floor plans.' Garden structures such as pavilions succumb to fire, often repeatedly, but their owners or the owners' descendants make it their business to restore or replace them as soon as this is possible. Never dismiss a Korean garden as somehow not genuine because some of its plantings or structures are new. This process of replenishment is part of a documented tradition which stretches back more than 1000 years and should be respected and valued.

Public Accessibility

Whereas most of the great gardens in Europe, Japan and China charge entry fees and have defined opening hours, a surprising number of Korean gardens, especially outside of Seoul, are open to the public at all hours of the day and for free. Even gardens listed on various cultural heritage registers are provided with simple bilingual signage and casual visitors may enjoy them unsupervised. Often you will be the only visitor and able to enjoy these venerable gardens in tranquillity. There seems to be no equivalent of the National Trust in the UK or the Archaeological Survey in India to fence off, protect, maintain and restore all types of Korean gardens. The main burden of maintenance of private gardens is often borne by the relevant clan or *jongga* (the head of families) with little or no assistance from the Korean government or charitable organisations, nevertheless the benefits may be enjoyed by all comers.

03 Spirituality and Korean Gardens

Long before the introduction from outside Korea of Daoism, Buddhism, Confucianism, Neo-Confucianism, and Christianity, Koreans had a rich tradition of folk belief, animistic worship and shamanistic practice. They also practiced a form of geomancy. Korean spirituality is richly syncretic. It is only slightly tongue in cheek to say that, when Koreans are surveyed about their religious affiliations, they add up to 130%. Therefore it can be difficult to separate out the religious and philosophical symbolism in Korean gardens and it is almost never possible to say: this garden is a purely Daoist garden or that garden is a purely Buddhist garden. The same symbols may represent different things in different religious traditions. They may also sit happily side by side in the most unlikely places. For example it is not uncommon for shrines to the old mountain gods or the three immortals to be found in Buddhist temple gardens. Nevertheless the more you are aware of the different threads of

Stones representing the pre-Buddhist mountain gods sit in the middle of the main entrance to a Buddhist temple in Busan. © Jill Matthews

religious and philosophical thought and symbolism underpinning Korean gardens, the richer your experience of them will be. Below is a quick sketch of the major threads. Later, specific examples of garden symbolism will be described.

Mountain Spirits and Immortals

Korea is a very mountainous country so it is not surprising that mountains have played a major part in even the earliest religious rites and observances. The belief that mountains are sacred, to be venerated and the home of spirits, immortals or enlightened ones, is deep-seated in the Korean psyche. It is central to the Dangun creation myth, is directly relevant to much shamanistic belief and practice, and sits comfortably with the later teachings of Chinese Daoism, Buddhism and Confucianism. Even in Neolithic times there is evidence that the tops of mountains were sacred and regarded as places of common sanctuary, owned by nobody, where competing or warring tribes could meet in peace, an ancient precursor of the concept of the public park or common.

Mountains are also essential to the practice of geomancy in Korea, as the providers of beneficial energy flows to important man-made sites.

Mountains are therefore regarded as excellent sites for shamanistic shrines, Buddhist temples, Confucian scholarly retreats, Daoist contemplation, palaces and family and official shrines. Many gardens of all kinds are sited either on mountainsides or to take advantage of views of particular mountains. Symbolic mountains are incorporated into many garden designs as man-made mounds, deliberate rock arrangements and as islands in ponds. Gardens are never constructed on the peaks of mountains and great care is taken to disturb the natural flow of water and the natural vegetation and the whole topography of mountains as little as possible.

Pungnyudo

Pungnyudo was a very ancient traditional set of Korean folk beliefs. The literal meaning of the word is 'wind-flow religion.' Adherents sought to attain truth or enlightenment by grasping the flow of life force and thus becoming immortal. One way to achieve this state was to enjoy nature, especially mountains and rivers, and to attempt to interact with the spirits in nature. Such ideas had obvious implications for the siting and design of Korean gardens and predisposed people to accept and practice later more formalised versions of geomancy.

Dangun Myth

The Korean creation myth is intimately bound up with a mountain and the theory of *um-yang* (*yin-yang* in Chinese terminology) and a primordial tree usually depicted as a Korean red pine. Dangun is reputed to be the semi-divine ancestor of the Korean people and the founder of the oldest, Gojoseon, dynasty which established its capital close to Pyongyang in North Korea in 2333 BC. There are several versions of this myth but they all commence with a divine city on top of Mt. Baekdusan and the union between a male divinity and a female human and consequent birth of Dangun. Dangun promised to improve the lots of the common people with the assistance of the wind god and the rain god. In all accounts he lived to a very great age on top of a mountain, often in the company of these two other 'mountain gods,' Hwanin and Hwanung. Mountain shrines were often built to honour the trio. It is therefore not surprising that when the quest of the early Chinese emperors to find immortality in the mythical islands off the coast of China or on various sacred and mythical mountains became known to the Koreans they easily incorporated it into their own cosmology. In fact when the first Chinese emperors sent expeditions of young boys and girls to find mushrooms of immortality on the tops of sacred mountains, the Koreans obligingly identified these mountains as Mt. Geumgangsan, Mt. Jirisan and Mt. Hallasan, all real mountains in Korea.

Geomancy (*pungsu*)

Westerners are more familiar with the Chinese term *fengshui*. In Korea similar practices and beliefs are called *pungsu* and they were employed in the selection

The Silla royal tomb park in Gyeongju is an example of site selection according to the principles of pungsu. The protective hills, copses of trees and placement of water all contribute to the excellent geomancy of the site. © Jill Matthews

of sites for major buildings and gardens from very early on in Korean history. Doseon, a Buddhist monk in the late Silla period (AD 827-898) systematised *pungsu* as a traditional geographical science quite different from Chinese *fengshui*. His theory was applied to the selection and to the preparation of auspicious sites by making up for weak or missing elements, minimizing overly strong elements and supplementing geographical energies especially by building Buddhist pagodas and planting copses of trees at appropriate places.

Pungsu was the dominant principle for the location and arrangement of man-made landscapes for the five hundred years of the Goryeo dynasty and greatly influenced the making of gardens during much of the Joseon dynasty. It is known that King Taejo, the first Joseon King, personally selected Hanyang, present day Seoul, as the site for his new capital and new palace because of its naturally perfect *pungsu*. Positive geomantic attributes of the site include: It is protected by mountains on the north, east and south; There is a space for the main palace on the foothill of southern slope of Mt. Bukaksan, overlooking the waters of Cheonggyecheon stream and the Han River to the south; The flat protected area in front of the palace would be ideal to build the new capital city; Some way from the front of the palace a lower hill would fence the city and a river flows from east to west, completing the *pungsu* requirements. However, despite these auspicious attributes, the most famous Korean, King Sejong, doubted the *pungsu* of the Gyeongbokgung palace itself and hence took care to live and die elsewhere in Seoul.

Pungsu principles can also have profound political effects. For example, in 1868 the desecration by a German adventurer named Oppert of the tomb of Daewongun, the father of the ruling Joseon monarch, was considered to have done such damage to the strength of the entire dynasty that it lead directly to their adoption of the closed door policy to the rest of the world and kept Korea isolated for many years.

During the colonial occupation of Korea by Japan between 1910 and

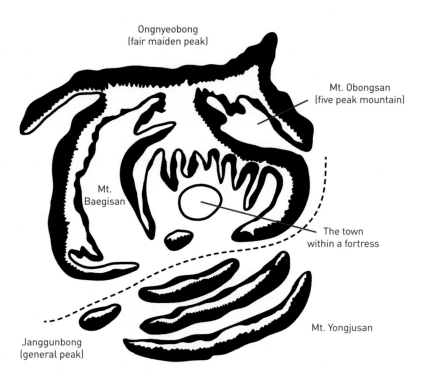

Ongnyeobong
(fair maiden peak)

Mt. Obongsan
(five peak mountain)

Mt.
Baegisan

The town
within a fortress

Janggunbong
(general peak)

Mt. Yongjusan

Elaborate diagrams drawn by *pungsu* masters, indicate auspicious sites for Korean gardens. Emphasis on protective mountains, correct orientation and permanent flowing water have assisted the survival of some gardens for hundreds of years.

1945 the Japanese rulers also took *pungsu* very seriously. The steps they took to disrupt the *pungsu* of the royal palaces and capital of Seoul are detailed elsewhere. To this day many Koreans believe that the Japanese forged hundreds of iron stakes and drove them into geomantically strategic mountain peaks and passes throughout Korea with the intention of disrupting the beneficial flow of energy though the whole of Korea and thus breaking the Korean national spirit. Regardless of the accuracy of this belief, now, more than 60 years after the departure of the Japanese, many Koreans spend much time and energy searching for any remaining stakes and removing and ritually destroying them, usually on August 15, Liberation Day.

Even in modern day Korea, correct selection of sites for graves, palaces, temples, shrines and their associated gardens, is considered extremely important. Aspiring Presidential candidates have been known to shift the grave-sites of their ancestors to enhance their chances of election and litigation concerning the position of grave-sites is not uncommon. The lovely modern Hee Won garden at the Ho-Am Art Museum in Yongin was laid out in accordance with *pungsu* principles and was built to honour Lee Byung-chul, the founder of Samsung whose grave is nearby.

Um-yang philosophy

Westerners are more familiar with the Chinese expression *yin-yang* and indeed the idea seems to have originated in China during the Warring States Period. However in Korea it is called *um-yang*. It is a theory of complementarity of opposites: sun/moon; masculine/feminine; active/passive; bright/dark etc. *Um-yang* theory is considered so important, that its symbolic representation, known as the *taegeuk*, is the central element on the Korean national flag. Combined with the theory of the five elements (wood, fire, earth, metal, water), it permeates almost all aspects of design and artistic expression in Korean culture, including garden design.

This *um-yang* symbol appears frequently painted on garden structures. Here it decorates the main doors leading to the garden of a Confucian academy.
© Jill Matthews

Shamanism

Shamanism has been present and its rituals practiced on the Korean peninsula for a very long time. It may well have come to Korea from the nomadic steppe tribes in neolithic times. Even in contemporary Korean society, shamanism is very influential and *gut* rituals are performed frequently for patrons seeking life advantages such as the recovery of health, the conception of children or the success of contemplated enterprises. Most shamans are women and the titles are semi-hereditary although some may train acolytes with ability, who are not blood relations. The respectful title for a shaman is *manshin*. Another term, *mudang* is no longer considered polite. The role of a shaman is to contact the spirit world and to channel individual spirits for the purpose of placating or interrogating them and mediating between them and the living.

Shaman rituals often occur on mountains or in the countryside or the domestic sphere, a practice no doubt encouraged by previous periods of repression, especially in Neo-Confucian times, when powerful women of any kind were usually frowned upon. Ironically, the belief that shaman could increase the chances of women to successfully bear children, ensured their survival during the late Joseon period when Neo-Confucianism decreed that the bearing of sons was crucial. Shamanism is generally regarded as a folk belief not shared by the elite. Some of the symbolism associated with it is irreverent towards authority, particularly Confucian and patriarchal authority.

The spirit most commonly channelled by Shaman in Korea is *sanshin*, a mountain spirit or mountain god. Shrines to *sanshin* may be found alone on mountainsides throughout Korea, but also in almost all Buddhist temples where they are often described as 'shaman shrines.' These shrines (*gak*) are usually small and sited at the back and the highest point of the temple compound where they are understood to evoke the protection of the mountain for the whole temple. They often contain paintings of the mountain spirit, usually accompanied by one or more tigers, and many symbolic objects and plants. Although *sanshin* was originally believed to be female, almost all paintings now depict the spirit as a kindly old man, sometimes in Confucian dress or with hands held in a Buddhist mudra position. Common plants depicted include the Korean red pine (*Pinus densiflora*) and peach trees and fruit. Frequently a single old red pine grows outside such shrines, just as they do next to the pavilions in scholarly retreat gardens, a venerable gardening tradition dating back to prehistoric times.

As is the way with syncretic Korean spirituality, elements of shamanism pervade the later more formal religions. When Chinese Daoism came to Korea, a form of shamanistic Daoism developed in which heaven and sacred mountains were both worshiped as shamanistic gods but with Daoist overtones. Later Buddhism, and even Confucianism, allowed elements into their rituals and symbols which acknowledged the mountain spirits, although often in a less exuberant style.

Shaman do not build gardens in the same sense as Buddhists and Confucians do, however their insistence on veneration of mountains, selection of auspicious shrine sites, and symbolic use of trees such as peaches and red pines in their art and ritual have indirectly influenced Korean garden design.

Chinese Daoism was first introduced into Korea in AD 624 during the Goguryeo period. This was not exactly news to the Koreans who already had *pungnyudo*, which shares many elements with Daoism. Daoists have several specific techniques designed to try to overcome death and become immortal and live on sacred mountains forever. Such beliefs reinforced the earlier more primitive veneration of mountains and affected garden design and symbolism in Buddhist temples and, more surprisingly, in Confucian scholarly retreat gardens during Joseon.

Buddhism

Buddhism first came to Korea from India via China in AD 372 during the Three Kingdoms period. By early in the Unified Silla era, it had become the state religion and remained dominant until the adoption of Confucianism by the Joseon dynasty almost one thousand years later. There was a second major wave of Buddhist influence with the arrival of *seon* (Zen or Pure Land Buddhism) from China in the eighth century. Under Unified Silla, attempts were made to assimilate the two schools of Buddhist thought, the original *Gyojong* or Doctrinal Buddhism with the newer *Seonjong* or Zen Buddhism. The result was a unique Korean form of Buddhism, which incorporated much of the symbolism and iconography of earlier Korean religions and spirituality, particularly beliefs in the sacredness of mountains and the old mountain gods and nature worship in general, and the practice of *pungnyudo*. These developments had profound effects on Korean Buddhist temple construction and of course on the gardens surrounding them.

Confucianism and Neo-Confucianism

Confucian thought arrived in Korea in two main waves beginning in AD 327 when it was introduced to the Goguryeo court. Initially, during the Three Kingdoms and early Goryeo periods, Confucianism and Buddhism were not felt to be incompatible. Buddhism was thought to deal with the metaphysical realm, whereas Confucianism dealt with conduct in the temporal realm. The early Confucian academies coexisted with the great Buddhist monasteries and the two gardening traditions continued side by side. As late as the nineteenth century an American missionary to Korea remarked, that 'the all round Korean will be a Confucian in society, a Buddhist when he philosophises, and a spirit worshipper when he is in trouble.'

The arrival of Neo-Confucianism during the late Goryeo period began to change this easy coexistence. Neo-Confucianism was not so accommodating of Buddhism and Korean society began to be reorganised according to Confucian centralised, patriarchal and hierarchical ideas. Finally, during the reign of King Taejo, the founder of the Joseon dynasty, Neo-Confucianism became the official state religion and remained so for the whole of the Joseon period, which lasted until 1910. Patronage of the Buddhist institutions declined as did the number of temples. The building of Confucian residential educational institutions such as *seowon* burgeoned throughout the countryside.

Most of the gardens that have survived to the present in Korea, date from either the Neo-Confucian Joseon period or the preceding Buddhist Silla period, so the effects of both Confucian and Buddhist modes of thought are significant for Korean garden design.

The effect of Confucian belief in the importance of social hierarchy on the layout of the gardens surrounding Confucian teaching institutions, palaces and tombs is explained in detail elsewhere, but Neo-Confucianism had several more subtle effects on gardens in Korea. Of central importance was the Confucian emphasis on education and in particular the introduction of the Chinese style civil service exam, which lasted for 1000 years. These exams guaranteed successful male candidates aristocratic, *yangban*, status. This came with feudal lands for themselves and their next three generations and so provided stability of tenure and the wealth and leisure necessary for the creation of significant and long-lasting gardens.

Familiarity with the Chinese literary classics, considered essential for a properly educated Confucian gentleman, contributed greatly to the literary allusions and calligraphy, which permeate most Korean gardens. It is likely that the elaborate and often lovely gardens of many modern university campuses in Korea are a contemporary echo of the Neo-Confucian emphasis on the importance of education.

Confucianism and Neo-Confucianism both place great emphasis on the relationship between ruler and subject: the loyalty expected of the latter and the reciprocal benevolence and upright behaviour expected of the former. The custom of creating scholarly retreat gardens became very popular during the Neo-Confucian Joseon period. Many were created by scholars and administrators exiled from or unpopular in the Court. Interestingly, some were created by men who went into self-exile, because they disapproved of the unregal behaviour of their monarch, a very Confucian judgement.

Many of these private scholarly retreat gardens lack the enclosed geometric formality of the gardens of Confucian educational institutions and royal palaces. Their design harks back to the earlier more asymmetrical natural layouts of their Buddhist Silla predecessors.

Confucianism had a second profound effect on Korean gardens. It enhanced and cemented the pre-existing historic clan structure in Korean society, thereby ensuring the survival of many old gardens. The tradition of the *jongga*, whereby the eldest son of each generation inherits the clan house and is obliged to maintain it as the cultural heart of his family, persists in contemporary Korea. Several hundred *jongga* continue to exist, often with family histories records and rituals reaching back for several hundred years. These duties include the maintenance of gardens built by or for illustrious ancestors of each clan. Many scholarly retreat gardens are restored and maintained by *jongga* as acts of Confucian filial piety and are open to visits by the public as a demonstration of clan pride and responsibility.

A third significant effect of Confucianism was the changes it brought to the role of women in Korean society. During Silla times, women were entitled to inherit aristocratic titles and land and thus could be independently wealthy. They also had access to education including to the Chinese classics. As Neo-Confucianism became entrenched, Korean women, even aristocratic ones, lost their rights and were slowly relegated to the domestic sphere and increasing illiteracy. There are no recorded instances of women building scholarly retreat gardens or endowing Confucian academies (*seowon*), during the entire Joseon dynasty. (One slight exception was the famous female scholar and artist, Shin Saimdang, who certainly had great influence on the plantings in her ancestral garden at Ojukheon described later.) Nor are there any signs that women participated in the elaborate literary rituals such as poetry writing in garden pavilions or extemporising verse at wine canal garden parties during Joseon, although they certainly did during the preceding Silla.

We should remember that while Neo-Confucian teachings concerning filial duty undoubtedly resulted in the preservation of many fine scholarly retreat and *seowon* gardens, these same teachings also resulted in the increasing exclusion of women from participation in the creation of gardens associated with Confucian beliefs and teaching.

Nevertheless during the Joseon period, royal women continued to support and endow several of the remaining Buddhist temples and their gardens and the two streams of Korean gardening tradition, Confucian and Buddhist, both continued.

Christianity

For purposes of completeness, it is necessary to mention Christianity as one of the spiritual threads in Korean society. Catholicism was introduced to Korea in the early seventeenth century and Protestant missionaries followed during the nineteenth. Partly as a consequence of the role of Christian missionaries played in resisting the worst excesses of the Japanese occupation during the twentieth century, Christianity has achieved a substantial presence in contemporary Korean society. It appears, however, to have had little influence on traditional garden design other than a misguided campaign to remove lotus from palace gardens in Seoul which will be described later.

04 Symbolism in Korean Gardens

Traditional Korean gardens may be appreciated in several different ways. Most obviously, it is a great pleasure to visit Korean gardens and simply enjoy their physical beauty. However if you dig a little deeper and learn to recognise some of the common symbols, your visit will be even more enjoyable. Old Korean gardens are packed with symbolism from animist, shamanistic, Buddhist, Confucian and Daoist traditions, often combined and sometimes even jumbled together. It is almost never possible to a say 'this garden is a purely Daoist garden' or 'that garden is a purely Buddhist garden.' The same symbols may represent different things in different traditions. Different traditions may also sit happily side by side in the most unlikely places. For example, it is not uncommon for shrines to the old mountain gods or to the three immortals to be found in Buddhist temple gardens or for Daoist ponds to appear in the gardens of Confucian scholars. Nevertheless, the more you are aware of the different threads of religious and philosophical thought and symbolism underpinning Korean gardens, the richer your experience of them will be.

Symbolic Rocks

The number and arrangement of rocks in Korean gardens is very significant in all these philosophic traditions. Commonly rocks appear

An arrangement of three rocks, a symbol common in gardens created before Confucianism ever arrived in Korea, appears in the garden of the Daegu Confucian Academy. © Jill Matthews

in twos, threes, nines or twelves, although there are occasional extravagant arrangements of sixty. Three rocks together may symbolise the three mountain gods in the Dangun Korean creation myth. On islands in ponds, they may also symbolise the three sacred mountains long sought by the Chinese emperors as the source of the mushrooms of immortality. Alternatively they may be seen as symbolic of representations of the doctrine of the three elements—heaven, earth and man. Arranged as two uprights with a capping rock they symbolise the *um-yang* principle, the uprights being the *yang* and the horizontal the *um* so that the whole arrangement symbolises the unity of the cosmos. It may be no coincidence that such arrangements echo the dolmen stones at the entrance to Neolithic gravesites throughout Korea or the rustic stone tables depicted in paintings of old Korean tea gardens.

Arrangements of twelve rocks have lusty connotations. Often appearing in royal gardens near wine canals and sites for parties and general merry-making, they symbolise the Mountain of Wu, which is an actual mountain in Sichuan province in China, which has twelve peaks. There is a popular Chinese myth dating back at least to the Warring States period, in which these peaks were said to be the abodes of twelve female immortals. In one version of the legend the Chinese King Xiang of Chu came to view the beautiful Mt. Wu, after which he took a nap and 'dreamed' he spent the night there with one of the female immortals which he enjoyed greatly and afterwards wrote ecstatic poetry wistfully recalling the encounter. As she departed next morning she told him she lived on one of the sunny peaks of Mt. Wu which she shrouded in cloud each morning and to which she summoned rain every evening. Consequently a shrine to the morning clouds was built on Mt. Wu and Chinese literature abounds with references to this titillating affair.

With their deeply ingrained love of mountains it is no wonder that Koreans have adopted the Chinese Mt. Wu myth almost as their own. Classical Korean literature has many references to 'the sunny side of the hill,' 'clouds and rain' and 'the dream of Mt. Wu,' all of which refer with varying degrees of delicacy to enjoyable, even immortal, outdoor sex. There are several gardens in Korea, which contain twelve symbolic peaks including the Imhaejeon Pavilion pond and the Wolji pond both in Gyeongju, and the Yongho Garden (Pearl Dragon and Tiger Garden) near Jinju in Gyeongsangnamdo province. So the next time you see an apparently random assemblage of twelve stones in a Korean garden, smile quietly to yourself because you understand the reference.

Korean garden makers rarely moved special stones over long distances and at great expense as happened in the making of Chinese gardens, however they certainly selected, named and ascribed metaphoric attributes to existing rocks on site. Occasionally a rock will bear a physical resemblance to its name such as the turtle rock in Buyongdong garden on Bogildo island, but more commonly the symbolic attribute is entirely abstract. A good example of this is the collection of more than sixty rocks in the pond in Seoseokji garden, none of which appear as anything other than insignificant ordinary natural shaped local rocks. Nevertheless each has a name, which refers to aspects of Chinese mythology, poetry or Confucian teachings or virtues. Together they form a sort of aide–mémoire or inspiration for visitors to the garden.

Ponds

Few Korean gardens are considered complete without at least one pond. We know this tradition was well established more

Leaping toad rock in Buyongdong garden on Bogildo Island is unusual because it physically resembles its name. © Jill Matthews

than 800 years ago because a beautiful Korean poem has come down to us, which describes a water bird landing in a square lotus pond. As well as their obvious aesthetic contribution to the overall design, these ponds are deeply symbolic. Square ponds containing a round island express the Daoist idea that the earth is square but heaven is round and by extrapolation the fundamental complementarity of the universe: creative and receptive, movement and stillness, active and passive. Confucians also viewed the universe as round and the earth as square, so square ponds with a round island may also indicate the garden of a Neo-Confucian scholar or even the presence of a Confucian academy. Buyongji pond in the grounds of Changdeokgung palace in Seoul is a good example of this type of pond. It is situated right next to the building in which the few successful examinees out of the hundreds who sat for the triennial Confucian civil service examinations were congratulated during the Joseon dynasty.

Ponds containing three islands are said to symbolise the Chinese legendary three islands of paradise or the mountainous abode of the three Korean immortals and thus the human search for immortality. The significance of rock arrangements on such islands has already been discussed but the

Symbolic ponds are central to most Korean gardens. Here is the lotus pond with a circular island in Yongho Garden. © Jill Matthews

presence and number of islands is also important.

Ponds in temple gardens are intended to inspire contemplation and to mark the boundary between the sacred and the profane. An excellent example of this holy pond is the beautiful oval one in front of the Bulguksa temple in Gyeongju which reflects the two bridges leading metaphorically to the Buddhist paradise beyond.

Groups of Three

It is remarkable how often things in Korean gardens come in threes: three islands in ponds; three trees on each island, three rocks on islands, three rocky outcrops on the banks of ponds or within view of pavilions or studies or meditation hermitages; three rocks forming tables; three rounded stones at the entrances to Buddhist temple gardens. Once you start looking, these trios are everywhere. Three has been an important number since prehistoric times in Korea as the numerous three-stone dolmen tombs show. It seems there were three mountain gods and three sacred mountains in Korea long before the Chinese emperors sent their expeditions to seek the three mountains of immortality and possibly before the Korean progenitor Dangun was born. He certainly took up residence on one of the three pre-existing sacred mountaintops in the company of two pre-existing mountain gods, thus making another trio.

Hence threes in Korean gardens can symbolise many things: the Chinese quest for immortality; the gods of the oldest religion; the three most sacred mountains in Korea; heaven, earth and man, and thus the essential wholeness of the universe. It all depends upon your own perspective and the context of the rest of the garden whether a particular trio is a Daoist symbol, a symbol of the old animist religion, a symbol of immortality, a graceful reference to Chinese mythology, or a reminder of the essential complementarity of the universe.

Levels

The relative levels at which structures in Korean gardens are built are very significant. By observing the height of the podiums on which they are built and how many steps lead up to them, it is possible to understand much about their importance. Thus in palaces, the King's bedchamber will be higher than the Queen's; in *seowon*, the shrine to Confucius will be higher than the scholars' hall; in Buddhist temples, the building housing the main Buddha statue will be higher than all lesser shrines and functional buildings such as dormitories and kitchens; and in aristocratic (*yangban*) domestic garden compounds, the master's study will be higher than the women's quarters.

In many gardens there are individual steps (*daetdol*) which are deliberately too high for normal progress, and are intended to emphasise transition from the mundane or profane world to different higher spheres such as sacred, royal, academic or masculine. *Daetdol* appear at the entrance to the Master's study in *yangban* homes, at the bottom of the normal steps leading to the King's chamber in palaces, and outside major shrines in temples.

Dismounting stelae (*hamaseok*) are found near the entrance to many gardens worthy of reverence or at least deference, including those surrounding royal or Confucian shrines, *seowon* and Buddhist temples. These stones originally indicated the point at which a visitor should get off his horse or out of his palanquin as a sign of respect for the teacher, deity, sage, king, or enshrined spirit within. Some suggest that the modern-day custom of getting off one's bike or out of one's car in order to greet an important person, such as one's professor on a university campus, stems from this *hamaseok* tradition.

Symbolic Trees

Many plants and trees in Korean gardens are there simply because they look beautiful or because they are useful, however many have additional symbolic meanings. The literary references embedded particularly in the sets of trees and plants, known as the 'four noble friends' or the 'three friends in Winter' are discussed in Chapter 5 (Literature and Calligraphy). Individual symbolic trees and plants, which appear frequently in all major types of Korean gardens are described here.

The **Korean red pine** (*Pinus densiflora*) is widely, if not officially, regarded as the national tree of Korea and plays many symbolic roles. Its Korean name, *sonamu*, means supreme tree. It is depicted in many representations of the creation myth. Single red pines also grow frequently next to the main pavilions in Confucian scholarly retreat gardens where they symbolise loyalty, constancy and righteousness because they remain green and do not shed their leaves in winter. They are planted outside almost every shrine to the shaman deity, *sanshin* or mountain spirit, in Buddhist temples. In the paintings within these shrines it is easy to recognise the *sanshin*, because *sanshin* is always accompanied by a tiger and a Korean red pine. This tree is also closely associated with royalty. As one of the ten symbols of longevity (*shipjangsaeng*), it is often depicted on throne and other palace decorations and is planted in vast numbers in royal tomb parks to express the wish for the perpetuation of the dynasty. Palace and temple buildings including garden pavilions are

A forest of Korean red pines lining the ritual walkway leading to a Buddhist temple. Pilgrims frequently deposit small stones as acts of piety before particularly noble specimens.
© Jill Matthews

Aged Korean red pines develop a fissured bark pattern which resembles the back of a tortoise, one of the symbols of longevity.
© Jill Matthews

Persimmons symbolise transformation. They are eaten fresh, dried and in tea.
© KTO (Korea Tourism Organization)

constructed almost exclusively of Korean red pine timber, no doubt for similar symbolic reasons.

Persimmon trees (*Diospyros kaki*) are widely cultivated in Korean gardens both for their fruit and their seasonal beauty. After a dazzling display of autumn foliage, persimmons lose their leaves but hold their brilliant orange fruits through many of the colder months. The sight of frost or snow limned persimmon branches with the fruit still tenaciously hanging from them is a very beautiful one. Because their fruit starts off hard, green and extremely bitter but ripens to a bright orange and becomes very soft and sweet, the persimmon is regarded as a symbol of transformation. As such it appears frequently in Buddhist temple gardens and both the fruit and its quadripartite calyx is often included in wooden carvings in temple buildings.

Ginkgo trees (*Ginkgo biloba*) are found in the gardens surrounding

Confucian schools and shrines all over Korea and are plainly associated with the great sage. Pairs of ginkgoes often mark the entrances to Confucian academies (*seowon*). Ginkgoes are said to shoot straight and fast towards heaven and thus to symbolise the fostering of many upright and high minded officials and their many fruits, the scholars who graduate each year.

The origin of the association of ginkgoes with Confucianism is the grave of Confucius in Shandong Province in China. During the eleventh century, the 45th lineal descendent of Confucius was renovating his grave and around it he planted many ginkgo trees. Ginkgoes continue to surround the grave and have since come to symbolise things Confucian and the achievement of probity and wisdom. Today in Korea they are frequently planted in all types of gardens to remind visitors of the virtues of the great teacher. Seen in this light the current choice for new tree plantings throughout the streets of Seoul of thousands of ginkgoes, may be more than just a pragmatic choice related to the ability of these beautiful trees to withstand modern day pollution.

A spectacular pair of ginkgo trees mark the entrance to the oldest and highest Confucian school and shrine in Korea, Munmyo Confucian Shrine, now a part of Sungkyunkwan University, itself the oldest in Korea.

One of the two five-hundred-year-old ginkgo trees at Sungkyunkwan University which survived its attempted destruction by the Japanese in 1592 and grew back stronger than ever. © Jill Matthews

The glorious golden Autumnal foliage of the Ginkgo once seen is never forgotten. A very fitting symbol for Confucian scholarship © Jill Matthews

As these ginkgoes were planted in AD 1519, they are approaching their five hundredth year. One of the pair was badly damaged during the sacking of the shrine complex by the Japanese in 1592 and is celebrated as much for its resilience as its longevity: it now possesses seven branches, which grew from the site of the injury, each as thick as the main trunk.

Plum trees appear in almost all types of Korean gardens, including royal palace, Confucian academy, scholarly retreat and Buddhist temple. It seems that the names for several different species of *Prunus* are translated into English as plum (or Japanese flowering apricot, just to be really confusing), of which the most common is *Prunus mume*. Long a favourite in both Chinese and Korean painting and literature, stylised plum blossoms represented as 5 or 6 white circles surrounding another, central white circle, appear often on the ends of ridge poles in garden buildings. These plum trees produce an astringent fruit, which can be made into a condiment, but are mainly valued for their pale fragile blossoms, which appear earlier than most other flowers, in late winter. What the blossoms symbolise is varied and complex: new year, the first month, purity, the end of winter, the ability to endure hardship, the Confucian ideal of ethical constancy in the face of adversity or

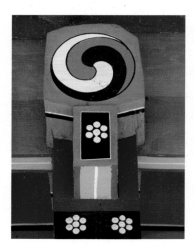

Stylised plum blossoms are a common feature in many garden structure decorations. © Jill Matthews

Fragile plum blossoms appear earlier than any other flowers at the end of winter.

even the sign of a principled recluse. Abstract depictions of plum blossoms were also closely associated with the Yi family, which produced many members of the Joseon dynasty royal family and so appear in the decorations in palace gardens.

Peach trees (*Prunus persica*) are also common in many Korean gardens and are appreciated for their blossom as well as their fruit. Daoists long regarded peach fruits as symbols of immortality and they are also regarded as symbols for spring, the third month and happy marriage. Representations of peaches abound in shaman shrines, Buddhist temples and palaces. Paintings of peach branches extending eastwards are believed to drive away evil spirits. Prunus trees in Korean gardens are of many types. The English words 'plum', 'peach' and 'apricot', are inadequate to translate the exact types of trees referred to in garden poetry.

Crepe myrtle trees (*Lagerstroemia*) were planted widely in the Joseon era, especially in scholarly retreat and Confucian academy gardens. Their Korean name, *baerong namu*, means 'flowers that last for more than 100 days.' The flowers symbolise the long lasting loyalty of humble Confucian scholars (*seonbi*) and the clean smooth bark, the integrity of such scholars. When you touch or tickle the trunk of these trees, their branches and leaves tremble which is seen as a metaphor for the sensitivity of *seonbi* towards the concerns of commoners. Despite their small stature and the delicacy of their flowers, crepe myrtles are

55

tough and quite long-lived with the older trees developing beautiful mottling colour on their smooth bark.

Symbolic Plants

The **Sacred lotus** (*Nelumbo nucifera*) is the most contentious of the symbolic plants commonly found in Korean gardens. Widely regarded as a Buddhist plant, the lotus grown in Korean gardens may indeed have originated in India and travelled to Korea with Buddhism itself, where it features extensively in temple iconography. Today, myriads of lotus-shaped paper lanterns are displayed in Korean Buddhist temples to celebrate the Buddha's birthday, statues of Buddha often sit on stylised lotus blooms and buildings are often decorated with carvings and paintings of lotus. However today the lotus occurs more frequently in temple decoration than in temple gardens, few of which have ponds appropriate for their cultivation. Moreover lotuses were also frequently planted in all types of Confucian gardens for hundreds of years, continuing until the present day. One of the most famous Confucian scholars, Toegye, who founded the Dosan Seowon, had a diminutive square lotus pond built beneath its lecture hall, for the better contemplation of the plant. He named the pond Jeongudang, which is a nickname for lotus. Lotus ponds continue to be major features in several other significant Confucian gardens including that of Korea's most famous poet Gosan (Yun Seon-do) on Bogildo Island; Seoseokji, built by Toegye's pupil Seokmun; and Imdaejeong woodland garden which has two lotus ponds, one for the usual pink coloured lotus and another for the rarer white blooming one. The two pavilion ponds in Gyeongbokgung palace, the main palace of the Confucian Joseon monarchs, were both conceived as lotus ponds and their names, Hyangwonjeong and the Gyeonghoeru, each refer to aspects of lotus cultivation.

Stylised lotus blooms, leaves and seed-pods are just as likely to adorn

Paper Lotus lanterns decorate the forecourt of a Buddhist temple in honour of Buddha's birthday.
© Jill Matthews

Confucian garden buildings as Buddhist ones. They abound on the newly restored buildings in the Gyeongbokgung palace complex, being most profuse and concentrated around the throne hall itself. It is therefore a matter for regret that misguided agitation by 20th century Korean Christians forced the removal of all lotuses from both of the pavilion ponds in

Stylised lotus decoration in a Confucian tomb park. Lotus is an important symbol in both Buddhist and Confucian gardens.
© Jill Matthews

Gyeongbokgung palace, on the spurious basis that they were 'Buddhist' flowers. Fortunately, after quite a few years, this misguided orthodoxy has been corrected and attempts are being made to reintroduce lotus once again into Gyeonghoeru.

The symbolism of the plant is obvious, not only to Buddhists and Confucians. It epitomises purity by arising clean from so much dirt and mud. It also represents creative power and the attainment of enlightenment. Do not confuse the lotus with all its associated symbolism with the **water lily** (*Nymphaea* sp.), which is also commonly grown in Korean gardens for purely aesthetic reasons and rarely if ever appears in the decorations of buildings or in Korean literary allusion. Lotus leaves, blooms and seed heads are all borne above the water on spiky stems whereas those of water lilies lie flat on the water surface. The stem attached to lotus leaf descends from the centre of an unbroken circular leaf whereas the stem attached to a water lily leaf is attached at the point of the split in the circular leaf.

Bamboo (*Bambusa* sp.) personifies the life of simplicity because it seemingly never produces flowers or fruit. It combines upright integrity with accommodating flexibility, bending in a storm but thereafter resuming its upright position and so copes well with adversity. Therefore it represents the perfect balance of grace and strength, or the *um* and the *yang*. Its hollow

Water lilies sit flat on the surface of the water, and have one split in their circular leaves. They are not particularly symbolic.

Lotus buds, leaves, flowers and seed heads sit well above the water surface on rough stems. Leaves are unbroken circles. Lotuses are one of the most symbolic plants in both Confucian and Buddhist gardens.

stems are said to represent open mindedness. Groves of bamboo are especially common in Confucian scholarly retreat gardens. There is a particularly fine example in Soswaewon garden in Damyang. Ojukheon garden described later even takes its name from the black bamboo which grows profusely in its garden.

Both **tree peonies** (*Paeonia suffruticosa*) and **herbaceous peonies** (*Paeonia lactiflora*), are widely cultivated in many Korean gardens where they are known as the Queen of flowers. As in China they are symbolically associated with royalty, especially queens, and are understood to symbolise honour, riches,

Bamboo, a favourite symbolic plant of Confucian scholars, here lines the entry to the famous scholarly retreat garden, Soswaewon. © KTO

Peonies, the queen of flowers, are common in royal and scholarly retreat gardens.
© Jill Matthews

Abstract representations of the striking seed heads of peonies are sometimes incorporated into carvings and paintings in garden buildings.
© Jill Matthews

love, affection and female beauty. They are often planted in flower terraces such as the one behind the queen's quarters in the Gyeongbokgung palace in Seoul.

Colours (*dancheong*)

The buildings in Korean gardens, particularly Buddhist temple and palace gardens, are frequently painted in bright harmonious colours. This practice is called *dancheong*, which means literally 'red and blue/green.' The traditional *dancheong* pigments were said to last for 1000 years, although more modern techniques modestly claim only a life of 100 years. Perhaps originally the practice had to do merely with the protection of the structural members such as timber columns, ceilings and roof struts from weather, fungus or insect damage. Certainly the traditional pigment giving the red colour contains cinnabar, a toxic compound containing mercury, which is a powerful fungicide and insecticide. But as long 2000 years ago during early Gogyureo, the five colours had also acquired symbolic meanings, each representing a cardinal direction: blue (east), white (west), red (south), black (north), and yellow (center). Also there were sumptuary laws concerning which social ranks could use the colours and on what buildings. Today the Korean state helps to support *dancheong* masters who are restoring palace paintings, and Buddhist monks continue to practice the art on their temple buildings. When visiting gardens with traditional structures illuminated by *dancheong*, do take the time to examine the paintings. Not only are the colours themselves beautiful, but many of the paintings are of symbolic plants. Lotus flowers, seed pods and leaves, plum blossom, persimmon and peach fruits abound.

An unusually elaborate *dancheong* panel with lotuses at a Buddhist temple. © Jill Matthews

Freshly painted *dancheong* at a Confucian King's tomb at Guri outside Seoul. © Jill Matthews

05 Literature and Calligraphy

Before 1446 when the Hangeul (Korean alphabet) was invented, the primary means of written communication in Korea was Classical Chinese. For many centuries it performed a similar role to that of Latin in Medieval Europe. Indeed it remained Korea's literary and administrative language until the start of the twentieth century. This is why most inscriptions, calligraphy and poetry found in Korean gardens to this day, are in Chinese characters. Almost every garden pavilion will have a nameplate and numerous wooden plaques with poems engraved into them, hanging within. Many rocks will have Chinese calligraphy engraved upon them, or at least be known to be symbols for Chinese mythic events, people or creatures. Later, gardens incorporated similar allusions to Korean folklore and traditions as well as Chinese, and some garden calligraphy began to appear in Hangeul.

These Chinese texts in Korean gardens are part of an elaborate and erudite

The naming of garden pavilions was central to the literary significance of the whole garden. Sometimes a king would grant a name-plate in his own hand as a great honour to the owner of the garden, as happened here in Dosan Seowon. © Jill Matthews

Poetry engraved in Chinese characters on a wooden plaques hanging in a garden pavilion. Distinguished visitors might be inspired by the garden to compose poems which were then preserved in this way. © Jill Matthews

game which allows people educated in this tradition to appreciate the gardens at a different, intellectual and literary level, in addition to that of solely aesthetic pleasure. For example, in the Soswaewon garden in Jeollanamdo province, there is a pavilion with a name-plate in Chinese characters which means 'Pavilion for Awaiting the Phoenix.' Visitors schooled in Chinese calligraphy and mythology would immediately realise the significance of the plantings which surround it: bamboo, reputedly the favourite food of the phoenix, and Paulownia trees, the favourite nesting place of these mythical creatures. Thus the whole garden can be read as a metaphor for Daoist ideas concerning the quest for immortality or alternatively as a place for a learned Confucian scholar to humbly await recognition of his intellectual attainments.

Sadly, fewer and fewer young Koreans learn classical Chinese calligraphy and literature these days, so they are unable to appreciate such references unassisted and thus their significance is slowly being lost. The older generation, justly proud of its literary heritage, has gathered together hundreds of these garden pavilion nameplates and poetry plaques in a museum near Andong at the Advanced Center for Korean Studies. This collection with many other significant Confucian printing woodblocks, was inscribed on the UNESCO Memory of the World List in 2015.

The tradition of embedding literary references into gardens, both by calligraphy and the cultivation of symbolic plants and by the naming of rocks and other natural features, began in China so early that there was already a best-selling book written in 1270 to assist would-be garden designers to select appropriate phrases, aphorisms and references. As with so many things, the Koreans took this idea and made it uniquely their own. The story of the encyclopedist Gwon Mun-hae, an official in the Court of King Seonjo, and his life's work, the creation of the *Daedong unbu gunok* (A Korean Guide for Writers also known as Korean Encyclopedia Sorted By Rhyme) is told with the description of his own garden, Choganjeong pavilion later in this book. He was working at the time of Shakespeare and Queen Elizabeth I in England and accessing and systematising a literary tradition that was already old.

Garden Poetry

Especially in scholarly retreat gardens it was customary for the owners to invite guests to write poems inspired by their experience of the gardens, which were then carved into wooden plates in various fine styles of calligraphy and hung in the garden pavilions. Even in translation, such Korean garden poetry has an elegant sparseness and brevity, often reading more like an aphorism or a haiku than a sonnet or a narrative epic. It also displays acute and detailed observations of nature, as one would expect from authors who spent much time sitting in open garden pavilions in beautiful surroundings with superb views to mountains and water. 'Lotus Blossom Pond' is a lovely example of such garden poetry. As it appears in the Collected Works of Minister Yi of Goryeo Korea by Yi Gyu-bo (AD 1168-1241), it must be more than eight hundred years old:

A lonely bird flies into a pond
Cutting through the water as though it were a piece of blue silk cloth.
A small wave ripples through the water in that square pond
Causing the lotus flowers on the surface to sway.

An example of the close relationship between gardens, literature and poetry is Imdaejeong pavilion garden in Jeollanamdo province. The name of the garden itself comes from a poem entitled 'Sitting Riverside Looking at Water, Thinking of Mountain' by a Chinese Song dynasty poet. The title of the poem is engraved in Chinese characters on the pavilion nameplate. The garden is a literal representation of its name: the pavilion sits on a mountain (actually a small hill) at the edge of a flowing stream, overlooks three ponds, and enjoys views to a distant range of hills. Within the pavilion are several wooden plates engraved with nature poems in Chinese, which refer both to the original poem and its manifestation in the garden.

The Four Noble Friends

Korean garden literature abounds with elegant references to symbolic sets of plants. The most common set is known variously as 'the four noble friends,' 'four gracious friends,' 'four gentlemen,' 'four noble plants' or the 'four gentlemen flowers.' The four noble friends are plum, orchid, chrysanthemum and bamboo. Another set of symbolic plants known as the 'three friends of winter,' are plum, pine tree and bamboo. This tradition began early in China where it was embedded in poetry, calligraphy and painting and even used to make subtle political statements in times of trouble and exile. Specific plants were widely understood to epitomise the virtues that Confucian scholars aimed to achieve: pine tree, bamboo and plum, which remain green or even flower in winter, signify moral tenacity under adverse conditions or alternatively steadfastness, and resilience; the chrysanthemum, which continues to flower long after all the other flowers of spring and summer, epitomises perseverance and fidelity; and the orchid, which exudes an exquisite fragrance in a remote secluded place, is like a humble scholar who does not self-promote.

Another set of four flowers, known as 'flowers of four seasons' are orchid, a symbol of spring, lotus a symbol of summer, chrysanthemum, that of autumn and plum, of winter. Together they symbolise the passing of the seasons and the great cycle of life dear to the hearts of Daoists and Buddhists. It is this literary and metaphoric overlay, which promotes the growing of this select group of plants in both Chinese gardens, and all types of Korean traditional gardens - Daoist, Confucian and Buddhist.

An excellent example of a 'four gracious friends' planting is central to Seoseokji, the famous Confucian scholarly retreat garden in Gyeongsangbukdo province. Overlooking the main pond is an elevated terrace with a rock proclaiming it to be a platform for four old friends. On it for 300 years have grown pine, plum, chrysanthemum and bamboo. Concerning it Jeong Yeon-bang, the original owner, wrote the following poem:

> *Plum and chrysanthemum stand out in a snow-covered landscape*
> *Pine and bamboo give nature colour after frost*
> *With pine, bamboo, plum and chrysanthemum as my friends in winter*
> *I will have companions as long as I live.*

Jeong Yeon-bang was not the first man of letters to group these plants together because of what they symbolise. Many earlier Chinese poems and paintings had done so. In fact Korean gardens share many symbolic plants with Chinese gardens because of their common literary and artistic heritage. Both Korean and Chinese poetry contain many references to plum blossom, chrysanthemums, pine and bamboo, and also to juniper trees, peonies, orchids among others. Gardens containing them, are intended to be considered as the embodiments of the virtues long associated with them.

Imaginary Gardens

Even scholars unable to create actual gardens could participate in this literary form of horticulture. The game known as *ui-won* was widely practiced during the late Joseon period. Scholars created perfect gardens in their imaginations and then shared them with their peers by means of poetry, essay or painting. As one Confucian scholar wrote:

I am too poor to have a big house and rich lands
And too sick to visit landscapes of beautiful mountains and valleys
An ui-won exists inside my mind
So, not even a painting is needed to enjoy it.

06   Chinese and Japanese Influences

Despite their unique qualities, Korean gardens have been influenced by Chinese garden culture and, in a mostly negative way, by the Japanese.

Chinese Influences

We have already examined the profound influence of Chinese literature and calligraphy on Korea garden design. In general Chinese influences were far more benign than those of Japan. Chinese cultural influences often came to Korea via dynastic marriage, trade/tributary visits between Chinese and Korean courts, and the teachings of travelling intellectuals such as Buddhist monks or Confucian scholars, rather than as a result of violent invasion and destruction. These influences may have been transmitted in both directions although there is little documentary evidence. Certainly both Chinese and Korean gardens have cultivated a common set of trees and flowers for their beauty and symbolic associations for many centuries including: plum, peach, apricot, pine, persimmon, pomegranate, ginkgo and juniper trees, and lotus, bamboo, peony, orchid and chrysanthemum plants.

Buddhism first came to Korea from India, via China. With the teaching probably came plants such as the lotus, now widely cultivated in many types of Korean gardens, and tea. Tea cultivation was long associated with Buddhist monasteries in Korea and many of them had their own tea gardens although none are known to survive today. With Confucian ideas from China came the reverence for ginkgo trees. The cultivation of juniper trees, originally for the making of incense, was probably a practice introduced from China. Daoist ideas from China emphasised the symbolism of peach and pine trees. In general the cultivation of symbolic plants to create a 'language of flowers' to make literary allusions was widespread in China before it was adopted in Korean gardens.

The very idea of scholarly retreat gardens originated in China, probably during the Warring States period when it was prudent for rich people to retire to the countryside until things settled down. Few such retreat gardens survive in China, except in Suzhou, but many are referred to in poetry and painting. Chinese scholars who could not build their own retreat gardens, played an elaborate 'parlour game' of imagining perfect examples of such gardens and representing them in poetry or painting. This Chinese tradition was continued and was elaborated into the *ui-won* among Korean Confucian scholars. Many surviving Korean gardens contain Chinese calligraphy, which mostly refers to classical Chinese literature and folk tales. Such calligraphy may be carved on rocks, pavilion nameplates or timber poetry plaques hung within pavilions. The gradual loss of understanding of this literary element of the gardens amongst modern-day Koreans, many of whom do not read or write classical Chinese, is unfortunate, but Korean gardens may be enjoyed in many ways, of which Chinese literary allusion is only one.

In addition to this rich literary influence, Korean gardens share several physical similarities with Chinese gardens. Elements such as pavilions, rock arrangements, wine canals, symbolic ponds and some plants appear in both, but in Korean gardens there is almost always a little twist which would make them seem out of place in China. An example is that the rooflines in Korean garden buildings have an elegant arc said to derive from a imitating a rice straw rope stretched but not too tightly, whereas Chinese garden pavilion rooflines are straight. Korean garden designers were selective in what Chinese influences they accepted. So for example they ignored the widespread Chinese tradition of transporting huge rocks long distances to build up imaginary landscapes, preferring to accept and enhance the local topography instead. Nor did they restrict themselves to the relatively limited array of symbolic plants cultivated in Chinese gardens. In addition to these they planted an ebullient array of flowers chosen simply for the pleasure they gave or the tenacity they displayed by surviving in a harsh climate with a minimum of fuss.

Japanese Influences

The principal influence of Japan on Korean gardens has been deliberate destruction. The Japanese have been so persistent in their efforts to destroy Korean garden culture, starting with the invasions between 1592-1598 (the Imjin Wars) and continuing through most of their occupation of Korea in the first half of the twentieth century, that this could be considered as an instance of attempted cultural genocide. It is almost impossible to visit an old garden in Korea today where the signage does not state with varying degrees of delicacy that it was partially or fully destroyed between 1592 and 1598 or, coincidentally, that its major trees were planted at that time, presumably because their predecessors had been cut or burnt down during General Hideyoshi's invasion.

At this time the Japanese captured many scholars, potters and other artisans including landscape designers and forcibly deported them to Japan where they enriched the developing Japanese garden and ceramic cultures, however it seems that the traditions of making tea gardens, tea cultivation and tea ceremonies, previously common in Korea, were obliterated by this huge loss of human capital. During the Japanese occupation between 1910 and 1945 the colonial administration had as its stated policy the total destruction of Korean cultural identity. In putting this policy into effect, the oppressors paid particular attention to the destruction of Korean gardens, which in retrospect only emphasises their symbolic power, uniqueness and special place in Korean culture.

One example of this stated policy was the complete obliteration of all gardens surrounding Joseon dynasty provincial government administration centres (*gwan-a*). All that remains of these once lovely gardens are scroll paintings of them made for administrative purposes, which survive in the archives of the Joseon court. Although of varying artistic merit, these scrolls clearly show that *gwan-a* had extensive gardens containing lotus ponds and pavilions, large trees, particularly ginkgoes and Korean red pines, and careful rock arrangements and terracing. One way or another they were all destroyed. Many were bulldozed and even their structural foundations buried. The buried remains of the *gwan-a* on Jeju island are presently being excavated and restored as an example of this lost class of Korean garden.

Another major example of Japanese influence on Korean gardens is the repeated deliberate destruction or mutilation of the five royal palace gardens in Seoul. All were totally destroyed during the Imjin wars in the sixteenth century, rebuilt by the Joseon monarchs only to be massively reduced again by the Japanese occupiers in the twentieth century. With the partial exception of Changdeokgung palace, the palace gardens we see today are mostly

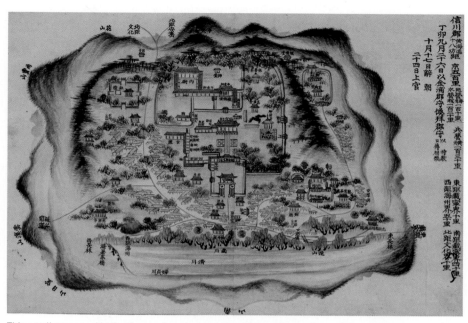

This scroll preserved in the Joseon dynasty court records is evidence of one of the many *gwan-a* gardens destroyed by the Japanese. Protected by hills on three sides and with water flowing below it, the garden contained many mature trees including willows, pine and plum, a lotus pond and viewing pavilion.
© Publishing Company Minsokwon

reconstructions made and replanted since the departure of the Japanese after the Second World War. During their occupation one secondary palace was completely destroyed, and one had all of its garden removed, with only a few buildings remaining. A number of 'accidental' fires severely diminished the Deoksugung palace and much of its landscaping was replaced by ugly un-Korean features such as an electric pump driven fountain in a concrete pond and a European neoclassic style palace now used as an art gallery. The secondary Changdeokgung palace where the Korean royal family was allowed to reside was also much reduced, although here it is still possible to get an idea of how the garden would have been before the occupation, and many old trees and water elements remain.

Gyeongbokgung palace, the principal Joseon palace, received special attention. Here hundreds of buildings were torn down, or removed to Japan or other locations in Korea. The main Japanese administrative building was deliberately sited so as to humiliate the last Korean monarch and destroy the geomantic energy of the palace. The nexus between the ritual altars and the ancestral Jongmyo shrine, was deliberately broken by the building of new roads. The Cheonggyecheon stream, which formerly flowed in front of the palace, enhancing the geomantic energy of the seat of Joseon government, was allowed to become a sewer before being covered over with another highway, further destroying its geomantic qualities. The stream was uncovered and completely restored in 2005. Today it provides a pleasant strolling route in downtown Seoul and, more importantly, it partly restores the geomantic energy flows relating to Gyeongbokgung palace. Finally hundreds of cherry trees, widely regarded as Japanese trees, were planted in the grounds, Japanese style pagodas were erected and, the ultimate humiliation, a zoo, was installed within the palace grounds.

So complete was the Japanese desecration of the palace gardens of Seoul that now it is difficult to imagine what they would have looked like in their glory days. Most of the palace gardens we see today are still in the process of reconstruction. The pride the Koreans take in this process and the effort and expense they make to restore their royal gardens are very understandable and should be seen as a great example of cultural resilience in the face of extreme adversity. The reconstruction of such culturally significant sites should also be seen as a great example of cultural continuity: this is not the first time they have been reconstructed. The tradition extends back for centuries.

There are documented historic examples of the export of Korean garden design expertise to Japan though no examples of transplants from Japan to Korea are known. Many of the same plants appear in the gardens of both countries and some architectural elements, such as the presence of wine cup canals in aristocratic gardens, originally a Chinese tradition, are similar, but overall the two gardening traditions are profoundly different. Korean gardens are not Japanese gardens, and owe nothing to them.

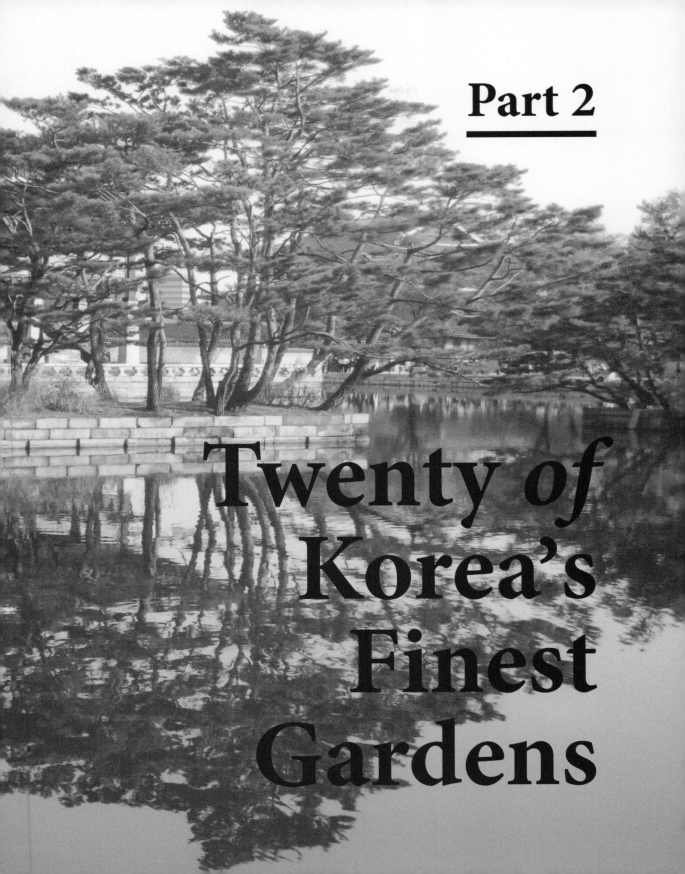

Part 2

Twenty *of* Korea's Finest Gardens

01   Palace Gardens

Introduction

Few traces remain of any of the palace gardens of Korean dynasties prior to Unified Silla, Goryeo and Joseon and most of these are in present-day North Korea and difficult to examine. It is known that the layout of the palaces of these earlier dynasties closely resembled those of their Chinese counterparts particularly the sixth century Tang dynasty capital in Changan (modern-day Xi'an). In China, this pattern was replicated for centuries up to and including the fourteenth century Ming capital palace known as the Forbidden City in modern-day Beijing. This style of palace is known as the East Asian style and was also copied, much later, in Japan.

However the Koreans habitually put their own stamp on everything, including palace architecture and gardens. As far as we know, early Silla dynasty palaces were much more naturalistic in style. By the tenth century Goryeo dynasty, variations on the East Asian style were appearing that are directly relevant to Korean royal palace garden design. The Goryeo kings put great emphasis on site selection and unlike the Chinese, ensured that their palaces were surrounded on all sides by protective mountains. Their palaces were constructed so as to preserve the topographical features of the site including the natural flows of water from the surrounding mountains. Palace buildings were oriented and shaped so as to maximise views to and emphasise the silhouettes of the nearby mountains. The palaces and their gardens were rarely built in the centre of their capitals. Neither city streets nor palace buildings were sited along straight axes, but rather they were built along the curving banks of streams or other existing topography. Palace walls were hardly ever rectangular. Instead they were irregularly shaped to better conform to the natural topography. Despite the constant threat of invasion and destruction, there was a marked reluctance to build walls at all. The palaces built during the Unified Silla period in their capital in Gyeongju appear not to have been surrounded by any walls. Even the later Joseon dynasty whose capital, Hanyang, became modern-day Seoul, only built an inner wall around the principal palace instead of the three walls usually constructed around their palaces by the Chinese. Instead of fortifying their capital and its palaces, during emergencies the Joseon court and some thousands of commoners would relocate to Namhansanseong fortress situated some 25km from the principal palace of Seoul. Namhansanseong contained within it a temporary palace far less grand than those in the administrative and ritual capital but was more easily defended.

In the early twentieth century there were five palaces in Seoul all dating from the Joseon era: Gyeongbokgung palace, Changdeokgung palace, Chang-gyeonggung palace, Gyeonghuigung palace and Deoksugung palace.

Of these Changgyeonggung palace contains some of the oldest surviving buildings and garden fragments. It may even be that some parts of this palace date from the previous, Goryeo dynasty. King Sejong, the fourth monarch of Joseon, lived there during the fourteenth century reconstruction of the nearby Gyeongbokgung palace, the main palace for the entire dynasty. Despite its reputedly perfect geomantic siting, the main palace was never a popular abode and most monarchs actually preferred to live in the secondary palace Changdeokgung palace.

During the Japanese occupation, Gyeonghuigung palace was completely demolished. The remaining four palaces were severely and deliberately mutilated and diminished by the Japanese colonial administration. Later they also suffered some damage during the Korean War. Today Deoksugung palace retains only fragments of its former gardens. A modern reconstruction of Gyeonghuigung palace is underway but it appears that it will have little garden surrounding it.

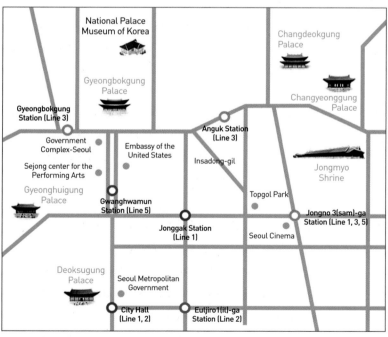

Location of the five royal palaces in Seoul. Changdeokgung palace and Changgyeonggung palace have the best preserved royal gardens.
© Cultural Heritage Administration

Changgyeonggung palace is adjacent to Changdeokgung palace and at times shared the Biwon garden with it although today they are separated by a wall. The gardens surrounding Gyeongbokgung palace and the Changdeokgung palace/Changgyeonggung palace complex, are the major palace gardens to be considered in this book. Gyeongbokgung palace is also presently undergoing extensive restoration and replanting but nevertheless definitely worth a visit. It is possible to purchase an integrated ticket to enable visits to the four remaining palaces and the Jongmyo shrine.

Changdeokgung Palace (especially Biwon meaning secret garden)

Name: Biwon (Secret Garden) also known as Huwon (Rear Garden) 창덕궁 비원(후원)
Location: 99, Yulgok-ro, Jongno-gu, Seoul 서울특별시 종로구 율곡로 99
Best Time to Visit: The garden is beautiful at all times of the year but autumn when the foliage colours are reflected in the ponds and Ongnyucheon stream, and spring when the cherry and plum trees bloom, are particularly wonderful.

The garden surrounding Changdeokgung palace is easily the most intact of the Seoul palace gardens. It is regarded as the finest Korean royal palace garden and comparable in significance to the Summer Palace garden in Beijing, China and the Katsura Imperial Villa garden in Kyoto, Japan. After its restoration in the late twentieth century it was entered on the UNESCO World Heritage List as an "outstanding example of Far eastern palace architecture and garden design integrated into and harmonized with the natural setting."

Changdeokgung and Changgyeonggung palaces occupy one large green space with the Biwon garden between them and for many centuries, were referred to together as 'the east palace.' Today the two palaces are separated by a wall and the Biwon garden can only be accessed by the public via

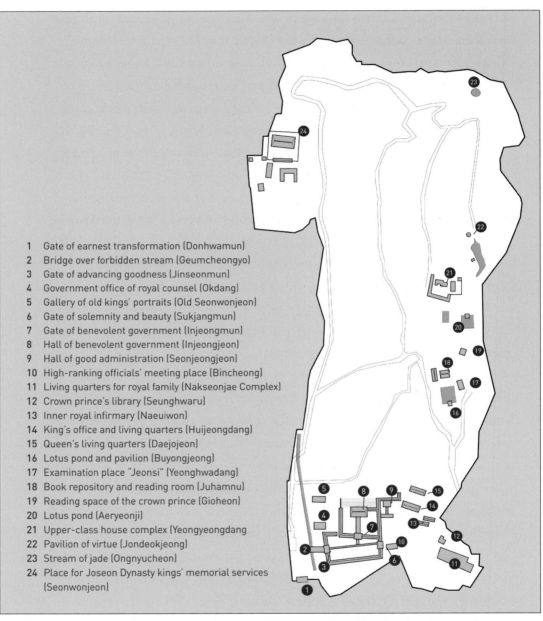

1 Gate of earnest transformation (Donhwamun)
2 Bridge over forbidden stream (Geumcheongyo)
3 Gate of advancing goodness (Jinseonmun)
4 Government office of royal counsel (Okdang)
5 Gallery of old kings' portraits (Old Seonwonjeon)
6 Gate of solemnity and beauty (Sukjangmun)
7 Gate of benevolent government (Injeongmun)
8 Hall of benevolent government (Injeongjeon)
9 Hall of good administration (Seonjeongjeon)
10 High-ranking officials' meeting place (Bincheong)
11 Living quarters for royal family (Nakseonjae Complex)
12 Crown prince's library (Seunghwaru)
13 Inner royal infirmary (Naeuiwon)
14 King's office and living quarters (Huijeongdang)
15 Queen's living quarters (Daejojeon)
16 Lotus pond and pavilion (Buyongjeong)
17 Examination place "Jeonsi" (Yeonghwadang)
18 Book repository and reading room (Juhamnu)
19 Reading space of the crown prince (Gioheon)
20 Lotus pond (Aeryeonji)
21 Upper-class house complex (Yeongyeongdang
22 Pavilion of virtue (Jondeokjeong)
23 Stream of jade (Ongnyucheon)
24 Place for Joseon Dynasty kings' memorial services
   (Seonwonjeon)

Map of Changdeokgung palace. The layout of both palace buildings and gardens follow the natural topography and the area of garden is greater than the area of palace buildings.

Changdeokgung but it is possible to visit both on a combined ticket. Some parts of garden may only be visited with a tour guide, so it is advisable to book.

Although Gyeongbokgung was always the official main palace and public focus of Joseon dynasty splendour and ritual, Changdeokgung was always the favourite palace residence of the royal family, members of whom continued to live here and enjoy the garden until the last Joseon Princess Deokhye and her Japanese sister-in-law Crown Princess Bangja, both died here in 1989. During their lifetimes there was a Japanese garden between the two royal ladies' residences but this was demolished immediately upon the death of Princess Banja. During the nineteenth century, a European style glasshouse was installed. Initially it contained exotics from all over the world but today it is stocked mainly with plants native to Korea. Many such enhancements, extensions and rebuildings were made at Changdeokgung by successive royal generations during its 600-year history.

Construction of the main Biwon garden began in 1406, during the reign of King Taejong, almost as soon as Hanyang (modern-day Seoul) was declared to be the permanent capital of the dynasty. For some hundreds of years no-one could enter the garden except at the invitation of the king. It was the private retreat of the royal family where they could relax, read, compose poetry, practice archery and calligraphy, go fishing or boating and admire nature.

Like all the palaces of Seoul, Changdeokgung suffered bouts of severe damage, usually by fire, mostly deliberately lit. All the buildings of the palace were burnt to the ground during the Japanese invasion in 1592, rebuilt, only to be largely destroyed again during King Injo's restoration in 1623. Several less damaging fires followed in the nineteenth century. Finally, major unsympathetic changes were imposed during the twentieth century Japanese colonial period including: the installation of new buildings created with materials from those demolished at Gyeongbokgung; the reduction in the number and changing of the shape of several ponds; the imposition of inappropriate roads; the planting of hundreds of cherry trees and the ultimate humiliation, the building of a zoo and cable car. Essentially the palace grounds became a public amusement park under Japanese occupation and this situation continued under President Park Jeong-hee. However today the zoo, cable car, the inappropriate roads and most of the cherry trees have been removed.

Despite these vicissitudes, the essence of the garden survives: we can clearly see the reverence for nature especially trees, the choice of plants which reflect the passing of the seasons, the widespread cultivation of native plants and trees, and the reluctance to interfere with the natural topography of the site. The proportion of buildings to the overall area of the garden is small and each building is situated and oriented to take advantage of a natural feature in the garden rather than aligned along an axis. Many elements of the garden have survived for hundreds of years: Jondeokjeong, one of the various elegant pavilions which are dotted along the main stream and on the banks of the several ponds, was built in 1644; the Geumcheongyo stone bridge was constructed in 1411; Donhwamun, the ceremonial entrance gate which was built in 1412 and reconstructed in 1609, and is the oldest original gate in Seoul. At the rear of several residential palace buildings, especially those occupied by various royal women are intact flower terraces (*hwagye*) recently appropriately replanted. The rectangular Buyongji lotus pond still contains its original circular island symbolising Heaven above the Earth. A wine cup canal where Joseon kings held drinking/poetry parties can still be seen and the Ongnyucheon stream continues to flow as it has for centuries from north to south, marking the boundary between the royal domain and the outside world and unifying the whole of the Biwon garden area.

The present palace covers an area of 110 acres (45 hectares) of which 78 acres can be regarded as Biwon, the former private royal garden. In former times

Spring lights up the 600-year-old Geumcheongyo bridge which marks the transition from the mundane outside world into the royal domain of Changdeokgung palace. © KTO

Garden pavilions from simple to sumptuous are one of the glories of Korean gardens. This is one of the several placed along the Ongnyucheon stream in the Biwon garden within Changdeokgung. © KTO

The small rice paddy where the king performed rituals to encourage good harvests for his people. © KNA

A Chinese juniper known to be at least 750 years old, supported in its old age by metal crutches, was probably planted for the purpose of making incense for the royal ancestors at the nearby Jongmyo shrine. © KNA

many species of practical value were grown here. There was a small rice paddy in which the kings performed ceremonies to ensure nationwide good harvests each season.

At one time it is believed there were 1000 white mulberry (*Broussonetia papyrifera*) trees in Biwon so that the royal ladies could cultivate silk worms and produce silk and thereby encourage commoners to do likewise. Only one ancient white mulberry survives now to remind us of this campaign. Today the garden contains thousands of trees of many different species, mostly ornamental, including at least 70 individual trees which are at least 400 years old. There is a Chinese gooseberry vine over 600 years old, a plum tree over 400 and a venerable Chinese juniper, which is known to have weathered 750 years. Korean gardening techniques do not include major pruning of trees so these old trees have been allowed to achieve their glorious full potential and then to fall into revered old age. It is notable that many species including Korean weeping willows (*Salix koreensis*), Japanese elms (*Zelkova serrata*),

Korean red pine (*Pinus densiflora*) and Japanese dogwood trees (*Cornus kousa*) are native to Korea, another attribute of Korean garden design established well before the modern western preoccupation with indigenous landscaping.

Gyeongbokgung Palace (especially Hyangwonjeong pavilion and pond and Gyeonghoeru pavilion and pond)

Name: Palace of Shining Blessing 경복궁, 향원정, 경회루
Location: 161, Sajik-ro, Jongno-gu, Seoul 서울특별시 종로구 사직로 161

Construction of Gyeongbokgung palace began in 1395 and for the 500 years of the Joseon dynasty, it remained the principal palace and symbolic centre of power. Much research went into the selection of the site, which was said by some to have perfect *pungsu*, because it is situated in a basin on the north bank of the Hangang river, ringed by mountains, protected at the rear by Mt. Bugaksan, and had a river flowing east west to its south. For a while the dynasty prospered and the heyday of the palace was during the fifteenth and sixteenth centuries. It was during these centuries starting in 1412, that Gyeonghoeru pavilion and pond, still a major feature of the palace garden today, were constructed. However the decision to build the palace on its present site was always contentious. After several political setbacks for the Joseon dynasty and the complete destruction by fire of the palace by the Japanese during the invasion of 1592, dissenting voices concerning the geomantic perfection of the site for the palace grew louder and it was not rebuilt for 273 years. Joseon kings chose to live, work and even die, at their other palaces in Seoul, principally Changdeokgung, just to be on the safe side. Eventually, commencing in 1868, Gyeongbokgung was reconstructed and became once again the centre of court politics and royal ritual and the king and court spent increasing amounts

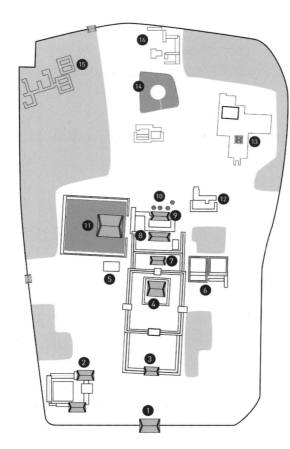

1　Main palace gate (Gwanghwamun)
2　National Palace Museum of Korea
3　Gate of spreading courtesy (Heungnyemun)
4　Throne hall (Geunjeongjeon and vicinity)
5　Government offices complex (Sujeongjeon, or Jiphyeonjeon)
6　Palace of the crown prince (Donggung)
7　King's office space (Sajeongjeon)
8　King's living area (Gangnyeongjeon)
9　Queen's living area (Gyotaejeon)
10　Hillside garden (Amisan)
11　Pavilion of joyous gathering (Gyeonghoeru pavilion and pond)
12　Living area of the king's mother (Jagyeongjeon)
13　National Folk Museum of Korea
14　Pavilion of far-reaching fragrance (Hyangwonjeong pavilion and pond)
15　Shrine for king or queen's coffin during funerals (Taewonjeon)
16　King and queen's living area (Geoncheonggung)

Map of Gyeongbokgung palace

of time in residence there. The palace buildings as reconstructed eventually formed a massive complex with 330 separate buildings standing on 4,657,576ft² (432,703m²) of land. During this period, in 1873, the other major water feature of the garden we know today, the Hyangwonjeong pavilion with its hexagonal islet and elegant bridge was constructed. Bad luck continued to dog even this lovely part of the garden because it was on a veranda of a new palace building overlooking the pond that Japanese assassins murdered the last Empress Myeongseong in 1895.

Geomantic energy and symbolism were understood by the Japanese colonial administration, only too well. Consequently they took special care to deliberately destroy both, by devastating Gyeongbokgung and its gardens. During their occupation, starting in 1911 they tore down 90% of the palace buildings. A few of the more significant ones were relocated elsewhere in Korea and some went to Japan where they were mostly destroyed during the Second World War. The beautiful main entrance gate to the whole palace area was first relocated and then demolished completely. In its place they erected a multistory Japanese Government General Administration block. Constituting the character for sun "*il* (日)" when seen from above, it was designed to put the stamp of the Empire of the Rising Sun on the peninsula and to overshadow the remaining palace buildings, humiliate the Korean Emperor and disrupt the *pungsu* of the whole palace site. Details of the various methods they used to disrupt the geomantic energy of all the Joseon palaces are described earlier in this book but in Gyeongbokgung palace they included the cutting down of many old trees which had survived the previous periods of dereliction and reconstruction and their replacement by hundreds of Japanese cherry trees and the installation of Japanese style pagodas. The destruction of Gyeongbokgung palace and much of its garden constituted a national tragedy.

However the Koreans have a long tradition of rising above such disasters. In 1989 almost as soon as the modern the economy recovered sufficiently from the Korean War and Japanese occupation, the South Korean Government commenced the process of restoration of Gyeongbokgung palace. On the fifth anniversary of the end of Japanese colonial rule they dynamited the offensive colonial administration building. Using traditional materials and craftsmanship Gwanghwamun, the main gate, has been reconstructed exactly where it stood originally. Water once again fills the stream-bed, which supplies the garden ponds. Inside the main gate visitors to the palace must cross this stream with its pretty bankside plantings on a reconstructed stone bridge and so be reminded that they are leaving the mundane world and entering the royal one. By the end of 2009, 40% of the buildings destroyed by the Japanese had been reconstructed, many adorned on their exteriors with beautiful *dancheong* paintings incorporating botanical symbols such as lotus, plum blossoms and bamboo. Major replanting is underway with thousands of new trees typical of traditional Korean gardens including willow, red pine, mulberry, dogwood, Korean mountain ash, juniper, prunus, maple and elm. Beds displaying more transient perennials, are appearing such as berberis, maybushes, asters, peonies, hog fennel, clover, chrysanthemums and various iris, many grown for their autumnal berries and leaf colours as well as their colourful blooms. Consequently good *pungsu* energy flows through Gyeongbokgung palace once more.

One of the many mature Korean red pine trees being transplanted into the restored Gyeongbokgung garden. The trunk and main branches are carefully swaddled with hessian and the whole anchored with strong guy ropes and supporting poles until the tree stabilises itself in its new position. © Jill Matthews

There are four main surviving features in Gyeongbokgung garden, which predate the present reconstruction. The first is the application of *pungsu* principles to the site selection and garden layout, which remains unchanged. The second is Gyeonghoeru pavilion and lotus pond now approaching its 600th birthday. The pond is square and contains the typical three islands on one of which stands the pavilion. It appears to float on the pond and creates an elegant reflection. Here the Joseon kings held banquets and boating parties for important foreign dignitaries, a tradition continued by South Korea's presidents. Surrounded by willows and with royal red pines on the other two islands, it is an austere, elegant and masculine compound.

Gyeonghoeru pavilion occupies the third of the three islands customarily built in such square garden ponds to symbolise the Chinese legendary three islands of paradise or the mountainous abodes of the three Korean immortals and thus the human search for immortality © Lily Matthews

Gyeonghoeru, the monarchs' personal compound within Gyeongbokgung, has an austere masculine appearance enhanced by winter snow. © KTO

The third old part of the garden, although more recent, is Hyangwon-jeong pavilion and pond. Compared to Gyeonghoeru, it has a much more feminine appearance. Originally it was joined by the longest wooden bridge in Korea to a part of the palace where the royal concubines lived. That bridge was unfortunately destroyed during the Korean War but has now been replaced by a brightly painted mainly concrete bridge on the opposite side. The hexagonal pavilion sits on a round island in the centre of the square pond surrounded by blossoming shrubs and with a lovely view of the water lilies, which decorate a large part of the surface of the pond. Many photos of brides and courting couples are taken around Hyangwonjeong.

The fourth significant garden feature also has strongly feminine associations. Amisan is a flower terrace (*hwagye*) situated immediately behind the Queen's quarters. It was designed to be viewed from her living room between painted screens depicting the twelve symbols of immortality. Amisan contains

Hyangwonjeong pavilion and pond in Gyeongbokgung palace. On the veranda overlooking this part of the garden the Japanese assassinated the last Korean Empress Myeongseong in 1895. © KTO

Amisan, the Queen's garden where plants emphasise the changing seasons and the twelve symbols of immortality abound both as living plants and ceramic representations. © KTO

four brick chimneys, which vent the ondol underfloor heating system. These are decorated with symbolic floral reliefs of bamboo and plum. There are also stone plinths for the display of interesting natural rocks. Plants on the terrace include peonies, day lilies, hostas, azaleas, dwarf peach and rhododendron, a selection which gives colour and pleasure in all seasons.

Apart from these three old areas most of the garden looks new, for obvious reasons, but time will put flesh on its bones and make it a celebration of

Some old trees survive in Gyeongbokgung including these twin apricots. Joseon monarchs were very aware of their symbolism and worried if blossoms appeared unseasonally. © KTO

Korean cultural resilience and national pride once again. Presumably Gyeong-bokgung palace will then join Changdeokgung on the UNESCO World Heritage List.

Donggung Palace and Wolji Pond Garden

Name: Donggung & Wolji 동궁과 월지
  (formerly known as Imhaejeon pavilion and Anapji pond 임해전 안압지)
Location: 102, Wonhwa-ro, Gyeongju-si, Gyeongsangbukdo 경상북도 경주시 원화로 102
Best time to visit: Autumn for the reflections of foliage in the pond, or Summer for the
  lotus blooms.

This palace garden was first constructed by the Silla King Munmu in AD 674 and thus is at least 700 years older than the oldest Joseon dynasty palace garden, Gyeongbokgung palace in Seoul. The garden originally surrounded Donggung, a secondary palace used by the Silla Crown Princes. Little of the original palace or garden other than the outline of the pond and the foundations of the various palace pavilions remain today, however after an extensive archaeological excavation of the palace site and dredging of the central pond, several of the palace buildings have been reconstructed and the original pond has been beautifully restored.

We know from written historic records that one of the three islands in the original pond housed a menagerie of exotic animals and birds. Boating parties were held and important foreign guests and national officials entertained on and around the pond. At one end there was a special canal where drinking parties were held and poetry extemporised. Nearby was an arrangement of 12 rocks representing Mount Wu, a real mountain in China, long associated with a rather lusty Chinese folk story. (See page 45 Symbolic

The asymmetrical layout of Wolji pond garden was typical of pre-Confucian gardens. The geometric lawn shapes indicate where palace buildings formerly stood. © Yonhap News

rocks in chapter 4 above.)

The layout of the garden was definitely in a more relaxed natural Buddhist style than later Confucian palace gardens. It seems King Munmu may have engaged the services of experienced Baekje dynasty garden designers to do the original design and layout. Baekje kings had been building beautiful gardens for at least three hundred years prior to commencement of construction at Wolji and although only tiny fragments of their gardens survive, it is nice to think that at least their design ideas live on at Wolji. The pond is very irregular in its outline. Indeed, the east bank, which is more than 1.3km long, has three ravines, several peninsulas and more than 20 curves, said to represent the spectacular scenery of the east coast of Korea, whilst the west bank where all the palace pavilions stood, was raised higher than the opposite shore to enable good viewing of the east bank from the 5 bankside palace pavilions. On the islands and on the east bank 1089 rocks were arranged deliberately, some standing, some lying, some jutting out over the water. Such arrangements are known as *suseok* and demonstrate Chinese

Wine canals such as this one at Wolji were common in the palace gardens of both Buddhist and Confucian monarchs. In Silla times royal ladies participated in wine canal poetry parties with the gentlemen. © Cultural Heritage Administration

influence in the design of the garden, however many other elements are said to be Daoist and Pure Land Buddhist in origin.

After the fall of the Silla dynasty the palace and garden fell into disrepair, although the pond survived for centuries and was known by the name Anapji. During the recent dredging and reconstruction of the pond a fragment of pottery was discovered on which was carved the name 'Wolji,' meaning 'pond reflecting the moon.' It is thought to have been the original name of the garden. Consequently the pond and garden are now known as 'Wolji' instead of 'Anapji.' This fragment and many of the thousands of artefacts found during the dredging of the pond in 1974 are displayed in the nearby purpose-built Wolji Hall in the Gyeongju National Museum and give further insight into this lovely and ancient garden.

Wolji is situated a comfortable walk from the Daereungwon Tomb Complex described in the chapter on Tomb Gardens. In summer there are great expanses of lotus to be enjoyed and in autumn the re-planted deciduous woodland reflect beautifully in the waters of the pond. The newly rebuilt

97

pavilions and the edges of the pond are now floodlit at night, perhaps a bit too stridently, but their reflections are spectacular. The restored garden is altogether a wonderful site for cultural performances and gives a good sense of how life used to be for the long-gone Silla courtly elite.

Some of the many rocks arranged on the East bank of Wolji pond. These included a set of 12 rocks representing the Mountains of Wu placed near the drinking canal, very titilating to guests with a knowledge of Chinese mythology. © Jill Matthews

The reconstructed Wolji pond and pavilions, floodlit at night, make a spectacular venue for contemporary cultural events. © KTO

02   Tomb Gardens

Introduction

No one familiar with the extensive landscaped grounds which surround the great aristocratic homes of England, such as Chatsworth House or Blenheim Palace, can fail to recognise the beautiful landscapes which surround the royal tombs of the Joseon and Silla dynasties in Korea as gardens on a grand scale. The tomb complexes of these two great dynasties have each been listed as UNESCO World Heritage sites. They are situated in and around the cities of Seoul and Gyeongju, respectively.

The kings of the Goryeo dynasty (AD 918-1392), which followed the Silla and preceded the Joseon dynasty, were buried in what is now North Korea, around Gaeseong, so we do not know how many of their tomb gardens have survived. Only a small number of royal tombs or fragments of royal tombs are known from other Korean dynasties such as Baekje (18 BC-AD 660) and

Goguryeo (37 BC-AD 688). None of these are surrounded by their original gardens. Therefore the tomb gardens which are considered here, all relate to either Silla or Joseon royal burials during the last 2000 years.

The royal tombs of the Silla dynasty are mainly situated in the city of Gyeongju in north Gyeongsangbukdo province, the site of its capital during Korea's golden age. There were 56 kings of the Silla dynasty, which was founded in 57 BC and lasted until AD 935. Hence all the Silla royal tombs predate the Joseon tombs of Seoul by several hundred years. Altogether 150 royal Silla tumuli tombs have been identified falling mainly into three clusters in and around Gyeongju. Known as the Great Tumuli Park, they form part of UNESCO World Heritage Site listing, *Gyeongju Historic Areas.*

Most of the Silla kings were Buddhist, so ancestral rites were not so important for them. Indeed it has not been possible to identify by name, the occupant of any Silla royal tomb. Nevertheless their tombs are treated with reverence, the landscaped parklands surrounding them are maintained scrupulously and the geomantic energy of their sites has been preserved despite the encroachments of the surrounding modern city. It is considered to be extremely poor form to climb onto any tomb mound, no matter how tempting the potential photograph might seem.

In contrast to Silla, the tombs of the Joseon royalty are much more constrained. While they retain the practice of burial under grass-covered mounds, these mounds are usually surrounded by stone balustrades and protected by larger than life human and animal guardian figures. Joseon tombs were clearly influenced by Chinese tomb practice and demonstrate a strict Confucian sense of hierarchy. There are 18 clusters of tombs containing 42 Joseon dynasty royal burials in and to the east and the west of Seoul. Together they comprise one UNESCO World Heritage Site: *Royal Tombs of the Joseon Dynasty.*

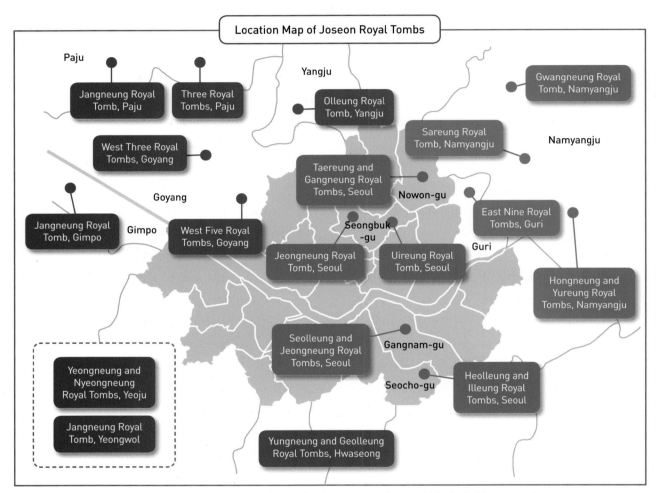

Location Map of Joseon Royal Tombs

Paju

Jangneung Royal Tomb, Paju

Three Royal Tombs, Paju

Yangju

Olleung Royal Tomb, Yangju

Gwangneung Royal Tomb, Namyangju

Sareung Royal Tomb, Namyangju

Namyangju

West Three Royal Tombs, Goyang

Taereung and Gangneung Royal Tombs, Seoul

Nowon-gu

Goyang

East Nine Royal Tombs, Guri

Jangneung Royal Tomb, Gimpo

Gimpo

West Five Royal Tombs, Goyang

Seongbuk -gu

Jeongneung Royal Tomb, Seoul

Uireung Royal Tomb, Seoul

Guri

Hongneung and Yureung Royal Tombs, Namyangju

Yeongneung and Nyeongneung Royal Tombs, Yeoju

Seolleung and Jeongneung Royal Tombs, Seoul

Gangnam-gu

Jangneung Royal Tomb, Yeongwol

Seocho-gu

Heolleung and Illeung Royal Tombs, Seoul

Yungneung and Geolleung Royal Tombs, Hwaseong

Location Map of Royal Burial Sites in and near Seoul. Together they constitute a UNESCO World Heritage site.

Korean Gardens

These places are actual burial sites and should not be confused with royal ancestral shrines, such as Jongmyo in Seoul where the spirit tablets relating to the Joseon kings and their families are housed, but the surrounding gardens are less extensive. At both the tomb sites and the ancestral shrines, elaborate ceremonies are still performed regularly by royal descendants as they have been for more than 500 years, except for a short interruption during the Japanese colonial period. Often these involve very old traditional styles of music and dance as well as the ritual preparation and presentation of food and drink offerings and demonstrations of obeisance. The ceremonies are themselves the subject of the UNESCO Intangible Cultural Heritage of Humanity Listing: *Royal Ancestral Ritual in the Jongmyo Shrine and Its Music.* The ongoing performance of the ceremonies together with the perfect state of preservation of the tombs and their gardens are very clear evidence of the continuing deep significance of Confucian traditions, in particular filial piety, in contemporary Korean society and constitute a remarkable example of cultural continuity.

Although the Joseon burials span a period of more than 500 years, the general layout of the tombs and their gardens is fairly uniform. The realm of the dead is clearly separated from the realm of the living, by a T-shaped building in which ritual offerings are made by descendants. Straight stone paths of differing levels for the living and the royal spirit, start at a red wooden gateway and lead to this building, but not beyond. The tomb is always higher than these other elements and covered with clipped grass and usually surrounded by symbolic stone figures.

The Joseon Court appointed special tomb guardians for each tomb cluster. This was a prestigious office and came with a luxurious home at the site and lands to provide income. Such guardians were responsible for the maintenance and protection of the tomb and its surrounding grounds, and were

103

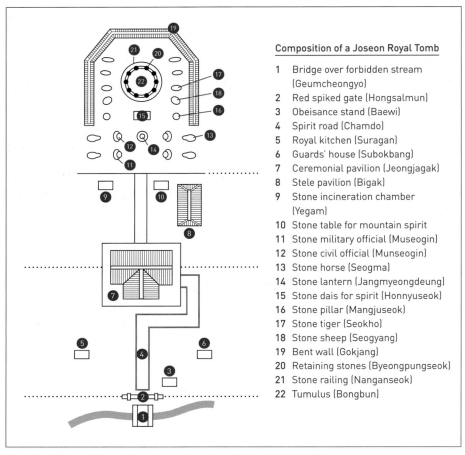

Composition of a Joseon Royal Tomb

1   Bridge over forbidden stream
     (Geumcheongyo)
2   Red spiked gate (Hongsalmun)
3   Obeisance stand (Baewi)
4   Spirit road (Chamdo)
5   Royal kitchen (Suragan)
6   Guards' house (Subokbang)
7   Ceremonial pavilion (Jeongjagak)
8   Stele pavilion (Bigak)
9   Stone incineration chamber
     (Yegam)
10   Stone table for mountain spirit
11   Stone military official (Museogin)
12   Stone civil official (Munseogin)
13   Stone horse (Seogma)
14   Stone lantern (Jangmyeongdeung)
15   Stone dais for spirit (Honnyuseok)
16   Stone pillar (Mangjuseok)
17   Stone tiger (Seokho)
18   Stone sheep (Seogyang)
19   Bent wall (Gokjang)
20   Retaining stones (Byeongpungseok)
21   Stone railing (Nanganseok)
22   Tumulus (Bongbun)

The typical layout of Joseon dynasty royal tombs varied very little for 500 years.

to ensure that appropriate rituals were performed in a timely fashion. Guardian residences, lovely traditional *hanok*, survive in at least two of the tomb clusters in Seoul and now house the modern day tomb administration and museums.

Despite these formal elements, Joseon tomb gardens share two important elements with those of the earlier and more relaxed Silla kings. Firstly, great care was taken to select the sites with perfect *pungsu* (geomancy), including protective hills behind and in front, water flowing to one side and maximum use of beautiful borrowed landscape. The tombs were built where they would be exposed to sunshine and not able to be flooded. Secondly, both types give the impression that they were inserted into an earlier sylvan tradition. Often they are placed within carefully maintained wild forests, complete with meandering streams and natural clearings with flowering meadows, which have become havens of biodiversity. Once a burial site was selected, all prior users of the land were removed and the forest declared the province of the deceased royal. It is not hard to imagine the influence on the surroundings of these tombs of the earlier animistic culture, which revered trees and believed mountains to be sacred.

When visiting tomb parks, it helps to understand the suffixes attached to the names of individual tombs, as they indicate the relative status of the occupants. The suffix '*neung*' or '*reung*' means tomb of a king or queen, '*won*' of a prince, princess or important concubine, '*myo*' that of other noble men and important commoners.

Donggureung Joseon Royal Tomb Park

Name: East Nine Royal Tombs 동구릉
Location: 197, Donggureung-ro, Guri-si, Gyeonggido 경기도 구리시 동구릉로 197

Seven Joseon kings, crown princes and other important members of the royal family are buried here, including the famous founder of the dynasty, King Taejo. Donggureung, meaning literally 'the nine royal tombs to the east of the capital,' is the largest cluster of royal tombs and the best to visit in order to understand the Confucian royal tomb landscapes. The whole tomb park occupies several hundred acres and in fact contains 13 tombs including several with multiple burials of kings and their queens. It takes several hours to fully

1 Sungneung (The tomb of King Hyeonjong and his consort Queen Myeongseong)
2 Hyereung (The tomb of Queen Danui, the first consort of King Gyeongjong)
3 Gyeongneung (The tomb of King Heonjong and his first consort Queen Hyohyeon and his second consort Queen Hyojeong)
4 Wolleung (The tomb of King Yeongjo and his second consort Queen Jeongsun)
5 Hwireung (The tomb of Queen Jangnyeol, the second consort of King Injo)
6 Geonwolleung (The tomb of King Taejo)
7 Mongneung (The tomb of King Seonjo, his first consort Queen Uiin and his second consort Queen Inmok)
8 Sureung (The tomb of the parents of King Heonjong)
9 Hyeolleung (The tomb of King Munjong and his consort Queen Hyeondeok)

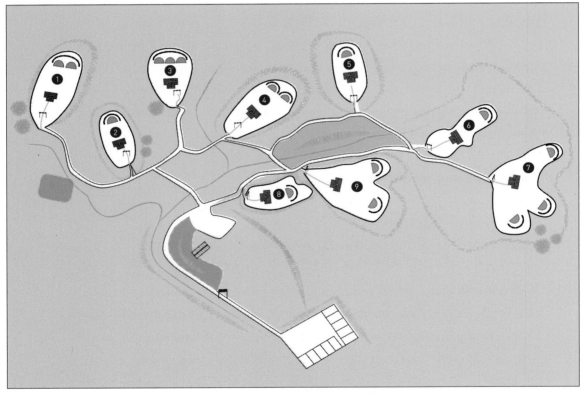

Map of Donggureung Joseon Royal Tomb Park where King Taejo, the founder of the dynasty, is buried surrounded by the tombs of 17 later kings and queens.

Korean Gardens

explore this tranquil garden and its sleeping occupants.

The burial mound of founder of the Joseon dynasty is a celebrated on a Korean 250 won postage stamp.
© Korea Post

The Joseon dynasty produced 27 kings during the 518 years of its history between its foundation in 1392 and its collapse in 1910. All but two of their tombs are situated in and around Seoul, which was the Joseon capital, then known as Hanyang. A regulation in Joseon's the oldest law book, the Grand Code for State Administration (Gyeongguk Daejeon) stipulated that all royal tombs should be constructed at least 4km outside the city gates but within 40km of them. This practical measure enabled subsequent generations to conveniently perform the necessary ancestral rites, so important for these Confucian monarchs and their descendants and subjects. Even youngsters learning their first Chinese characters from a Joseon dynasty text book (*Saja Sohak*), were exhorted: Conduct memorial services with the utmost care to pay tribute to your ancestors and respect your roots. Such rites have been conducted in the tomb park at Guri for 600 years with a brief interruption during the Japanese occupation and Korean War. At present, they are performed by the Jeonju Yi Clan Association on the anniversary of the death of each occupant. Such ongoing demonstrations of filial piety no doubt contribute greatly to the survival of the tombs, which are all intact, and to the preservation of their surrounding park landscapes.

It is easy to see the significance of site selection at Donggureung where the surrounding forest streams and landscape remain fairly undisturbed by modernity and the clever use of borrowed lanscape is not impeded by the encroaching metropolis. Many mature trees, both deciduous and evergreen,

107

make your visit a pleasure whatever the season. Deliberate clearings throughout the woodlands allow herbaceous perennials and bulbs to thrive. Preponderant species among the conifers are Korean red pine (*Pinus densiflora*), referred to as *sonamu* in Korean, and considered a symbol for longevity long associated with Korean royalty. These dominate the protective forests behind each tomb and appear often at each side of the red-spiked gates that mark the entry to each tomb area. In fact the tomb buildings are constructed and repaired with red pine timber which in past times would have been harvested from the surrounding forest. There are no straight avenues here. Paths and woodland follow the natural contours of the site until each tomb is reached, and visitors emerge into the sunlight and a vast expanse of clipped grass and follow (but do not step on) the spirit path to the ritual shrine and upward view to the actual tomb.

The later tombs cluster, each in their own clearings, around that of the founder of the dynasty, King Taejo. Of him a poignant story is told. He wished to be buried in his home village, quite a distance from Seoul. His wish was not granted. Instead, on the orders of his son, special rush-like grasses from the home village were brought to Donggureung and planted over his tomb. This act of filial piety by his son and the importance of King Taejo, as the founder of the dynasty, is celebrated by the recent issue of a postage stamp. To this day, six hundred years later, his is the only tumulus which is covered with uncut grasses, their seed heads waving in the breeze and catching the sunlight.

Burial mound of King Taejo planted with reeds from his father's ancestral village by his filial son.
© National Research Institute of Cultural Heritage

The geometric formality of a Donggeureung tomb is set amongst managed forest and meadows from an earlier sylvan tradition. © Jill Matthews

The beautiful gardens surrounding the historic tomb cluster Donggureung are popular for school excursions. Children respond to both the informality of the shaded flowing streams and woodlands and to the solemnity of the tombs.
© Jill Matthews

Funerary buildings and decorations at Donggeureung have been maintained, and appropriate rituals have been performed, by filial descendants in a tradition almost unbroken for 500 years. © Jill Matthews

Tomb-keeper's house at Donggureung. The position of royal tomb-keeper was very prestigious, came with a good house and income and could be inherited. © Jill Matthews

Silla Dynasty Royal Tomb Parks

Name: Daereungwon 대릉원

Location: 9, Gyerim-ro, Gyeongju-si, Gyeongsangbukdo 경상북도 경주시 계림로 9

The capital of the Silla dynasty for hundreds of years is now the site of the city of Gyeongju in Gyeongsangbukdo province where many royal burials are situated. Within the actual city are three main tomb clusters, which together form part of the UNESCO World Heritage Listing: *Gyeongju Historic Area*. Of these clusters Daereungwon is the largest. Here are 23 tumuli tombs, two of which when excavated, revealed thousands of valuable and beautiful artefacts now housed in the nearby museum. The tombs themselves can be visited.

Silla tombs are unadorned tumuli, covered only with mown grass. No attention is paid to symmetry or enclosure of either the individual tombs or the surrounding gardens. There are no processional pathways or avenues and no apparent hierarchy in terms of height or size. Water features, while present, had not assumed the symbolic significance and design centrality apparent in later Joseon era burial parks. Each tomb is sited to borrow landscape from the surrounding hills and to echo their shapes. They nestle companionably near each other creating a feeling of calm, dignified harmony. Copses of trees, especially Korean red pines, are dotted amongst them. Other trees such as ginkgoes, persimmons and crepe myrtles mark the passage of the seasons but are only planted sparsely. The whole effect is of wide, open created parkland, which must have been unusual in a time when Korea was almost fully forested. Perhaps the Silla burial parks are an unconscious homage to the distant origin of the dynasty in the far off grass-covered steppes of Central Asia. These kings and queens were buried with birch-bark saddles, sometimes even their horses, and their golden crowns were decorated with leaf shapes found also in the

Asymmetrically sited and echoing the shapes of the surrounding hills, the Silla tombs in Gyeongju are best viewed in the late afternoon light. © Suh Jae-sik

An unknown Silla king and his queen lie here, their tranquillity undisturbed by the surrounding modern city. © Jill Matthews

artworks of the Siberian steppes. In life it would have been easy for the kings of Silla to ride their horses through the lightly wooded, open spaces between the tombs of their ancestors in Gyeongju.

Seolleung and Jeongneung Royal Tomb Park

Name: Seolleung and Jeongneung (Seon-Jeongneung) 선릉·정릉
Location: 1, Seolleung-ro 100-gil, Gangnam-gu, Seoul 서울특별시 강남구 선릉로 100길 1

Situated within easy walking distance of Seoul's vibrant Gangnam area and the COEX Mall, these three tombs are perhaps the easiest of the Joseon royal tombs to visit in Seoul. Now entirely surrounded by high-rise buildings, the tombs and their surrounding tranquil parkland are a little known but wonderful green lung in the midst of one of the most densely packed and frenetic parts of Seoul.

Here lie King Jungjong, the eleventh Joseon monarch and King Seongjong, the ninth monarch and his queen. Their tombs are known as Seolleung and Jeongneung respectively and the whole area as Seon-jeongneung. They are part of the UNESCO World Listing: *Royal Tombs of the Joseon Dynasty*. Near the entrance to the tomb park, there is an excellent History Centre which shows the elaborate arrangements made to bury a Joseon monarch and the ongoing rituals necessary to be performed by his descendants. The three tombs follow the typical layout of Joseon royal burials described above with red arrow gate, spirit path, ritual pavilion, grass-covered tumulus tomb surrounded by stone balustrade and anthropomorphic figures and protected in the back by a forest of predominantly Korean red pine trees.

Despite the formal layout of the tombs themselves, the parkland and forest surrounding them are surprisingly naturalistic. It is almost as if this new, geometric Chinese style of tomb, has been inserted into a much older sylvan landscaping tradition. Despite being right in the midst of Gangnam, they are set in several acres of beautiful woodland. There is a flowing creek, meandering pedestrian paths through a Korean red pine forest, broad-leaved trees, and carefully created clearings within which shafts of sunlight encourage vivid patches of low-growing flowering herbs. The presence of large numbers of red pines is significant because they are one of the ten symbols of longevity and their evergreen nature was understood to symbolise loyalty in Confucian times and a wish for the perpetuation of the dynasty. Walls of red pines back each tomb: deciduous trees predominate along the meandering pathways. The whole tomb park is enclosed by a modern fence, thus discouraging shortcut walk-through traffic, and much effort is made to maintain it by removing senescent trees, planting and tending replacement trees, controlling exotic weeds, watering in drought times, keeping the grass covering the tomb mounds trimmed and so on. It is an altogether tranquil and dignified space utterly

There are only three royal burials in the Seon-jeongneung tomb park but they and their surrounding landscape remain intact and provide a peaceful escape from one of the busiest parts of Seoul. © KTO

Peaceful Autumnal strolling in Seolleung & Jeongneung Royal Tomb Park, an oasis in downtown Seoul. © KTO

Korean Gardens

removed from the throbbing materialistic hubbub that surrounds it. Many people visit to walk or to sit quietly under the trees, but there are no loud music, BBQs or riotous sporting games. No one climbs the tomb mounds which are clearly regarded with quiet reverence.

Each guardian figure has a different face and perhaps represents a real life courtier. © Jill Matthews

Stone guardian figures, balustrade and walls separate the tomb from the more naturalistic red pine forest behind. Confucian Joseon dynasty tombs are more formal in character than the older tombs of the Buddhist Silla kings. © Jill Matthews

Korean Gardens

Autumn in Seon-Jeongneung. Despite its apparently naturalistic style, the forest is obviously curated so that deciduous trees do not surround each tomb. © KTO

Three formal paths leading towards a royal tomb in Seon-jeongneung each at different levels, the highest for the spirit of the king, the second for his descendants as they perform rituals in his memory and the lowest for visiting commoners who are expected not to walk on the stone paths. © Jill Matthews

03   Buddhist Temple Gardens

Introduction

The gardens surrounding Buddhist temples are some of the oldest in Korea, many with histories stretching back more than 1000 years. Most are situated in unspoilt mountainous areas, which are, themselves, a pleasure to climb or walk in and have been declared to be national parks. Entry fees charged at the entrances to these parks help subsidise the upkeep of the temples within them.

It is difficult to select only three Buddhist temple gardens as being Korea's finest, because so many temples have significant and interesting gardens. There are the twin **Woljeongsa** and **Songwonsa** temples in Gangwondo province with a two and a half hour woodland walk between them and their impeccable flower meadows; **Tongdosa** temple in Gyeongsangnamdo province, the largest in Korea, with kilometres of ritual walkways on elegant boardwalks along the banks of streams, over stone bridges through cultivated forests between its

The six hundred-year-old Korean red pine which was granted the high rank of *jeongipum* by King Sejo for services rendered. © Suh Jae-sik

numerous hermitages; **Songgwangsa** in Jeollanamdo province with its superb rainbow bridge and the centuries old pair of entwining Chinese junipers; and **Beopjusa** temple in Chungcheongbukdo province with its unique 600-year-old pine tree, which was invested with the very high royal rank of *jeongipum* by King Sejo in 1464 after it obligingly elevated its branches to allow him to pass in his palanquin on his way to visit the temple.

Nevertheless a selection must be made, so later we consider Haeinsa, Bulguksa and Unmunsa temples in some detail. There are many common attributes in these three and most other temple gardens.

Entry pathways to Buddhist temples

Pilgrims and visitors to the temples are encouraged to approach them on foot up ritual pathways, which usually meander through managed forests.

Although these trees are obviously selected and tended, they are rarely planted in straight avenues but rather are less formally arranged in the older, more sylvan, tradition. Many of the oldest trees will have heaps of pebbles forming little pagodas, deposited within the crevices of their roots by pious pilgrims. These ritual pathways are never straight and always lead uphill, and so could be seen as a metaphor for the difficult progress towards enlightenment. Often they cross symbolically cleansing flowing water more than once on stone bridges, and they usually pass through several gateways. The number varies from temple to temple but commonly there will be an *iljumun* or 'one-pillar gate,' a *geumgangmun* or 'diamond gate' followed by a *cheonwangmun* or 'four heavenly kings gate.' Much has been written about the significance of these gates in Buddhist cosmology but the point to grasp in relation to temple gardens is their role in marking the symbolic transition from the secular to the religious or spiritual, on the 'path' to enlightenment. Along the pathway between them you may find pagodas said to contain relics of the Buddha or funerary stupas containing the ashes of famous monks associated with the temple.

One of the three gates on the ritual walkway leading to Songgwangsa temple. © Jill Matthews

At the end of the ritual walkway there is often a tranquil reach of water crossed by an arched or rainbow-shaped bridge such as the lovely one leading into **Songgwangsa** temple in Jeollanamdo province. Another example is the triple arched bridge crossing the sacred pond in front of the famous **Bulguksa** temple in Gyeongju. It may not be too fanciful to suggest that these bridges and their reflections may be metaphors for the passage from the prosaic and ephemeral outside world into the contemplative higher realm inner world beyond. Of course the great Buddhist temples all have vehicular access for delivery of essential services and the halt and the lame, but it is no accident that tourist car and bus parks and food and souvenir shops are situated at a considerable distance away from and below the temples and their gardens. The whole process of walking up to a Buddhist temple through beautiful, peaceful woodland or forest is designed to be a calming meditative and mind-clearing process through a sacred landscape, and should be experienced as such.

The exact mix of trees found along the ritual pathways is influenced to some extent by climate and geography. Thus **Woljeongsa**, in the high mountain

Pilgrims have scattered many votive pebbles along this ritual walkway. © Jill Matthews

Ritual walkways to Buddhist temples are rarely straight and always lead uphill.
© Jill Matthews

Two bridges crossing the cleansing flowing water on the ritual walkway leading to
Songgwangsa temple. The symbolism is emphasised by the abstract lotus carvings on the
balustrade. © Jill Matthews

area of Gangwondo province, is surrounded predominantly by fir trees whereas temples further south tend to have forests with many more broad-leaved and deciduous trees. **Bongjeongsa** temple in Andong in Gyeongsangbukdo province has an oak forest, **Haeinsa** temple in Gyeongsangnamdo province has a mixture of Korean red pine and deciduous trees and **Songgwangsa** temple in Jeollanamdo province is surrounded almost entirely by deciduous trees. However there is no doubt that nature is assisted in her selection of forest trees surrounding Buddhist temples to encourage splendid stands of both useful timber and symbolic trees. Most Buddhist temple buildings are wooden and require constant renewal after fire or other damage. It is not uncommon when visiting temples to hear the sound of sawing, chopping or hammering or to smell the beautiful smell of fresh cedar or pine sawdust in the air, as this process of temple building and renewal continues.

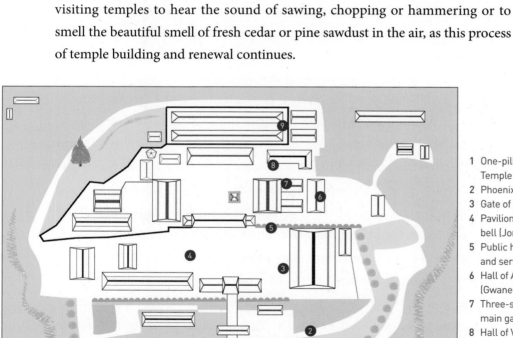

1 One-pillar gate to Haeinsa Temple (Iljumun)
2 Phoenix gate (Bonghwangmun)
3 Gate of liberation (Haetalmun)
4 Pavilion with Buddhist temple bell (Jonggak)
5 Public hall for Buddhist prayer and sermons (Gugwangnu)
6 Hall of Avalokitesvara Bodhisattva (Gwaneumjeon)
7 Three-story pagoda in a temple's main garden (Jeongjungtap)
8 Hall of Vairocana Buddha (Daejeokgwangjeon)
9 Hall of Tripitaka Koreana (Janggyeongpanjeon)

Map of Haeinsa temple (Typical layout of Buddhist temple garden)

Geomancy (*pungsu*)

The siting and construction of early Korean Buddhist temples were modelled closely on those Chinese temples and followed Chinese *fengshui* principles. However after the arrival from China of second great wave of Buddhist influence known as zen and the formal teaching of Daoism, the Koreans developed their own unique form of Buddhism known as *seon* or Pure Land and with it their own unique set of geomantic principles known as *pungsu*. Most surviving temples in Korea date from this second wave of Buddhist thought, which meant they were built in secluded mountainous areas intended to enhance opportunities for meditation and pilgrimage and to be far from the royal seats of power. Their gardens demonstrate techniques for minimising evil energies and strengthening weak ones known as *bibo pungsu*. Groves of trees were planted at strategic points around the temples to block evil energy flows. A perfect early example of such siting of a pagoda is to be seen at **Mireuksa** temple in Jeollabukdo province. *Pungsu* principles mandated that the temples and their gardens should be sited on the lower slopes of significant mountains, be protected on three sides by other mountains, always have permanent sources of flowing purifying water and should do as little damage to the original topography of the site as possible. No one who has had the good fortune to be present at one of the great Buddhist temples at dusk and to listen to the temple-closing chants and drumming will ever forget the experience. As the clouds roll down the surrounding protective mountains like the closing curtain of a dramatic performance and the music reverberates through your own body and the whole valley, you will be in no doubt that the application of these *pungsu* principles leads directly to the creation of profoundly beautiful temple gardens. All of these geomantic principles, first applied to Buddhist temple gardens, were later applied to palace, tomb and Confucian scholarly gardens throughout Korea.

Flower terraces (*hwagye*)

Once inside the temple complex, you will often be surprised by the profusion of colour and transient plants in many of the garden beds. Often the retaining walls which support each courtyard level, are softened by narrow flower terraces, known as *hwagye*. Usually these contain short-lived annuals and biennials and sometimes a few perennials: evening primroses, hydrangeas, cosmos, day lilies, grannies bonnets, pinks, irises, various daisies and narcissus, peonies, chrysanthemums, azaleas, clover, hostas and Boston ivy. It is said that monks and nuns particularly favour hydrangeas because of their neutral gender and subtle misty flower colour. Otherwise there is no discernable colour scheme other than a near absence of white flowers. Well planted *hwagye* make a lovely contrast to the stone, tile and rammed earth of the retaining walls at all times of the year.

Flower terraces growing small plants and shrubs known for their seasonal displays such as lilac, azalea, hosta, lily and camelia are a common decorative element in Buddhist temple gardens. © Jill Matthews

There is not a strong association between Buddhist temples and traditional herbal medicine comparable to the role of European monasteries in Medieval medicine. The main object of the selection of plants in these flower terraces seems to be to mark the changing of the seasons and perhaps to re-enact "the birth-life-death cycle." This may be because Daoism arrived in Korea at roughly the same time as Buddhism was becoming established on the peninsula and the two modes of thought were synthesised into the uniquely Korean form of Buddhism. The essentially transient nature of the bedding plants, is reinforced by the choice of shrubs and small trees elsewhere within the temple grounds. Crepe myrtles, viburnums, plums, magnolias and maples abound, all famed for their seasonal glories. Some temples such as **Songgwangsa**, even feature hardy banana trees (*Musa basjoo*) on their garden terraces. These must die back each cold winter, but re-grow each spring. They are said to symbolise the transience and emptiness of life because of their hollow stems. Often they are planted conveniently close to meditation halls so that the sound of rain falling on their broad leaves can calm distracted minds.

Otherwise within the temple complexes there are few trees, possibly because of the ever-present threat of fire. Each platform or court may have one or two conifers, maples or crape myrtles, sometimes pruned to restrict their size and growing in small island beds amidst large areas of swept paving or crushed stone.

Flower meadows

Although several other types of Korean gardens may include flower meadows, it is in temple gardens that they are seen most commonly. **Unmunsa** temple in Angang maintains a large area of cultivated exotic flowers such as peonies punctuated by statutes and walkways and **Woljeongsa** temple has an expanse of daisies under-planted with wild strawberries, however the more common practice is to create clearings in the surrounding forest in which diverse native flowers and ground covers are encouraged by removal of shrubs, exotic weeds and shading trees. Such areas abound with wild creatures including butterflies and bees and provide a sunny tranquil contrast to other areas of the garden. Sometimes they are the site for memorial stelae for famous monks of the temple but often they are just delightful clearings in the woodland where diverse nature can be enjoyed in peace.

Lack of enclosure

Some Buddhist monasteries can trace their history back at least 1400 years. Although no individual structures or gardens have survived this long, many have been rebuilt and replanted on the same sites, often repeatedly. **Songgwangsa** temple for example, has had 6 major reconstructions and is currently undergoing another, following its complete destruction during the Korean War last century. The practice by some monasteries of training fighting monks to defend the homeland from invaders no doubt contributed to this pattern of destruction and resurrection. In these circumstances it is surprising that Buddhist temples are never fortified or even enclosed. The gardens simply shade off into the surrounding forest and it is almost impossible to discern where cultivation ends.

Shrine to the mountain god

Most Buddhist temple complexes include a shrine to the pre-Buddhist Shaman deity, *sanshin*, which literally translates as 'mountain spirit.' These small stand-alone buildings (or *gak*) usually stand high at the back of the temple complex against a background of red pines. They commonly house a painting of an old man invariably accompanied by a tiger and a red pine. Indeed any painting of a sage figure, male or female, whether in Buddhist or Confucian garb, when accompanied by a tiger and a red pine, is almost certain to be of a *sanshin* recluse who has retreated from the outside world seeking enlightenment and immortality.

Lotus Iconography

Lotus is both cultivated and represented in many Confucian gardens, however it is in Buddhist temple gardens that its symbolism is most widely employed. Buddha statues often sit on representations of lotus flowers. Temple buildings are frequently decorated with paintings and carvings of all parts of the plant: bud, bloom, seed heads, leaves, even cross-sections of the root tubers. Buddha's birthday is widely celebrated by decorating temple courtyards with hundreds of paper lotus blossoms lanterns, the mindful creation of which is regarded as a form of meditation.

Other botanical decorations

While lotus symbols abound in temple decorations, other plants are also depicted. When visiting their Buddhist buildings, look up. The screens, structural rafters, ceilings and canopies within the major halls are often superbly decorated with carvings and paintings of numerous symbolic plants. A glorious example is the ceiling in the Jeokmyeolbogung hall of **Tongdosa** temple, which is covered with three-dimensional bands of richly painted peony plants and chrysanthemum blooms.

Bulguksa Temple Garden

Name: Bulguksa Temple (Buddhist Land Temple) 불국사
Location: 385, Bulguk-ro, Gyeongju-si, Gyeongsangbukdo 경상북도 경주시 불국로 385
Best time to Visit: Autumn when the maples and ginkgo leaves are reflected in the

pond in front of the temple entrance and the multitude of deciduous trees in the surrounding forest are in their full colourful glory.

There has been a temple at Bulguksa for more than 1400 years. Today the temple is one of the head temples of the Jogye Order of Korean Buddhism, an amalgam of doctrinal, Zen and Pure Land Buddhism, which incorporates uniquely Korean elements such as reverence for mountains, Shamanism and Daoism. With its associated hermitage, which houses the famous Seokguram Buddha, Bulguksa has a UNESCO World Heritage Listing as one of the world's cultural assets. The main temple contains eight listed national treasures including pagodas, bridges and Buddha statues, and is one of the most widely visited in South Korea.

A small temple was constructed on the site in AD 528 during the Three Kingdoms period, but construction of the temple we see today began in earnest under the kings of the Unified Silla dynasty in 751. There were at least 40 stages of building and renewal during the next 1300 years even during the later, Confucian, Joseon dynasty. One particularly major renewal was required after the deliberate destruction of every wooden structure in the temple complex during the Japanese invasion of 1592. It commenced in 1601 and another major restoration, after the end of Japanese colonial occupation and the Korean War, began in 1979. Despite this almost constant process of renewal, Bulguksa is regarded as a masterpiece of Silla architecture and design because, as far as is known, each renovation followed closely the eighth century layout and the foundation walls and platforms are original. This is quite a remarkable example of cultural continuity in the face of adversity.

Bulguksa is situated in a place with excellent geomantic properties on the lower slope of Mt. Tohamsan, within a beautiful forest and with permanent streams running down the mountain on either side. Its construction demonstrates one of the most fundamental elements of Korean landscape

Bulguksa temple nestles into Mt. Tohamsan, following its contours. The ritual pathway can be seen, passing the surviving pond with its central island. The distribution of autumnal colours demonstrates the cultivated nature of the forest surrounding the temple. © KTO

design: rather than carving out level ground from the roots of the mountain, the whole temple is built on artificial platforms based on foundations comprising huge hewn columns of stone infilled with intricate arrangements of natural or only slightly dressed granite boulders. Thus no damage was done to the integrity of the mountain by the construction of the temple, which nestles into the natural contours of the mountain flank. These foundation walls, still standing after more than 1000 years are beautiful in themselves and add greatly to the harmony of the whole temple.

The sacred landscape surrounding the temple complex is a garden lover's dream, not least because so many of the trees and plants, both familiar and unusual, are labelled with their names in English and Latin as well as Hangeul. To visit the temple one must first walk up the ritual pathway. The main temple garden lies along this pathway and is more interesting than the plantings within the temple complex itself. Unusually, the pathway is not dominated by three gates. Instead their symbolic function seems to be filled by a series of bridges and stairways. The loveliest bridge, one rainbow-shaped with three arches, crosses a large irregularly shaped pond fringed with willow, maple and ginkgo trees. In it there is an island with pine trees and a swathe of water iris. Except on very windy days, this bridge is reflected in the tranquil surface of the pond and can be read as a metaphor for the crossing from the mundane and transient outside world to the more solid realm of spiritual enlightenment within the temple.

These granite foundations of Bulguksa temple ensured no damage was done to Mt. Tohamsan by the construction of the temple. Such reverence for mountains and reluctance to change natural topography are fundamental principles in Korean garden design.
© Jill Matthews

Originally there were three ponds on the ritual pathway. Now sadly, the one immediately at the entrance to the temple is dry. Previously the temple buildings and the fringe of grand ancient Korean red pines would have been reflected in this pond but nowadays pilgrims must content themselves with traversing one of the two stairway bridges. Known respectively as Blue Cloud bridge and White Cloud bridge. Both designated as national treasures, their

The famous rainbow bridge at Bulguksa temple that marks the transition of visitors into the spiritual realm of the temple.
© Jill Matthews

symbolic message of progress upwards towards enlightenment is clear despite the present lack of water underneath. Within two of the temple courtyards the garden continues. Here only smaller trees and many shrubs and plants prosper, mostly displayed in stone walled flower terraces, carefully separated from the wooden temple halls because of the risk of fire. Azaleas, chrysanthemums, iris, viburnums, native perennials, small prunus, cherries, plums and maples cheer the visitor in all seasons. Many of the trees and shrubs are labelled in English, Latin and Hangeul, a real educational bonus.

The ritual pathway continues past the main entrance to the temple to the famous Seokguram Buddha Grotto, a distance of four kilometres and not for the faint hearted on very hot or cold days, however the cultivated forest through which it meanders is a pleasure to experience in more benign seasons.

In former times this paved entry into the main Bulguksa complex would have been a pond in which the temple would have appeared to float. The old Korean red pines are probably survivors of islands in that lost pond. © KNA

Unmunsa Temple Garden

Name: Unmunsa Temple (Cloud Gate Temple) 운문사

Location: 264, Unmunsa-gil, Unmun-myeon, Cheongdo-gun, Gyeongsangbukdo
경상북도 청도군 운문면 운문사길 264

Best Time to Visit: Spring for the azaleas or Autumn for the maple colours.

Unmunsa temple was founded in AD 560 during the Silla period and so has a history spanning almost 1500 years. It is the largest Buddhist nunnery in Korea, in which approximately 250 nuns practice for four years at a time. Perhaps it is this female element that makes the garden subtly different from those at

Unmunsa temple is one of the oldest in Korea and one of the few nunneries. The site has perfect geomantic properties. © KTO

other Buddhist temples in Korea. From a geomantic point of view the temple is perfectly sited, on the southern end of the Mt. Taebaeksan at the foot of Mt. Unmunsan with the clear Unmuncheon River flowing to one side, in the midst of a deep forest of Korean red pine and fir trees. In addition to the main structures and formal gardens, there are five smaller satellite temples in the surrounding temple forests - Sariam, Naewonam, Bukdaeam, Hogeam and Cheongsinam. These may be reached on foot along beautiful forest pathways. As is often the case with Korean Buddhist temples, the car park is placed at a distance and visitors are intended to walk along the lovely ritual walkway to approach the temple. Unusually this pathway lacks the usual three symbolic gates.

The nuns cultivate several acres of vegetable garden on the flat land approaching the main entrance and a large meadow garden within the main temple grounds. Here in season you will find: spirea, peonies, day lilies, camellias, plum blossoms and numerous bulbs and ground covers. Careful

Unmunsa's 500-year-old weeping pine tree with abstract lotus stone ablution fountain. © KTO

Despite the ever-present risk of fire in the precious Unmunsa temple buildings, the grounds immediately surrounding them contain a pleasant wisteria pergola, an ancient pair of ginkgos and several other significant trees. The main cultivated flower meadow is close by. © Jill Matthews

succession planting ensures colour in the garden for most months of each year. This garden shades off into the surrounding forest, which comes alive with azalea blooms in spring and vivid maple foliage in autumn. Closer to the main buildings, one finds a series of pergolas covered with wisteria and other flowering vines and several isolated old trees. These include a grand pair of ginkgos, but pride of place, near an elegant lotus fountain, is a marvellous old pendulous red pine tree (*Pinus densiflora f. pendula* Mayr), designated Natural Monument No.180. Reputed to be more than 500 years old, it is fertilised each spring with 216 litres of Korean rice beer (*makgeolli*) during a very ancient ceremony.

Haeinsa Temple Garden

Name: Haeinsa Temple (Temple of the Ocean Mudra) 해인사

Location: 122, Haeinsa-gil, Gaya-myeon, Hapcheon-gun, Gyeongsangnamdo

경상남도 합천군 가야면 해인사길 122

Best time to visit: The woodland surrounding Haeinsa temple has many deciduous trees which display glorious autumnal colour.

Haeinsa is recognised as one of the three jewels amongst Korean Buddhist temples, the other two being Tongdosa and Songgwangsa. Haeinsa has existed since AD 802, when it was endowed by the fortieth Silla King, Aejang. The temple and the famous Tripitaka Koreana within it are on the UNESCO World Heritage List. Almost alone amongst Korean Buddhist temples, Haeinsa

Sited to capture prevailing dry winds and avoid damp winds, Haeinsa temple is entirely designed to achieve the continued preservation of the Tripitika Koreana. © KNA

The main role of Haeinsa temple is the preservation of the thousand year old Tripitika Koreana. © KTO

emerged unscathed from widespread destruction during the Japanese invasion between 1592-1598. It had another lucky escape in 1951 during the Korean War when, because it was believed that 1,000 North Korean soldiers were sheltering nearby, the Allied forces dispatched four bombers to destroy them and Haeinsa. Fortunately the Korean leader of the mission knew of the existence of the Tripitaka Koreana and disobeyed his orders, thus saving both it and the temple. Seven other major accidental fires have damaged some of the temple buildings over the years but fortunately none have damaged the Tripitaka.

The Tripitaka Koreana is a set of 81,258 woodblocks carved with 52,382,960 beautiful, uniform and faultless Chinese characters and is the most complete set of Buddhist sutras, precepts and other literature, in the world. It is more than 1000 years old and was created as a national project to be a talisman against further invasion by the Khitan and Mongol peoples. The project took 12 years to complete and involved the cutting down of 15,000 trees and the efforts of more than 1.3 million Koreans in the gathering and curating the Buddhist scriptures, transporting the timber, preparing the wooden blocks, engraving them and preserving them. The blocks were intended to enable the printing of copies on special long-lasting mulberry paper called *hanji*. Visitors to Haeinsa may still purchase their own copies of selected pages printed in the traditional manner on *hanji* from this extraordinary treasure. Haeinsa temple, its surrounding landscape and the Tripitika are together listed as a UNESCO World Heritage site.

Because of its role in preserving the Tripitaka, Haeinsa's garden is slightly unusual in its layout. Firstly the temple and garden are oriented south-west so as to capture the prevailing dry winds but avoid the damp winds that come from the southeast. Rather than the usual one stream or river, Haeinsa has a river and two other streams flowing around it. Thirdly, the precautions taken to prevent damp, mould, and insect and fire damage, and ensure perfect ventilation, limits the number and types of plants in the courtyards immediately surrounding the buildings in which the woodblocks are stored. Nevertheless, the garden at Haeinsa is significant. Within the temple there are several lovely flower terraces, some planted with deciduous shrubs such

In every season the flower terraces of Haenisa temple soften the elegant retaining walls of the temple, often with surprisingly ebullient colours. © Jill Matthews

Monks, pilgrims and tourists on the ritual walkway to Haeinsa temple. © KTO

as viburnums, magnolias and maples, even a surprising stand of banana trees, and under-planted with flowering bulbs, chrysanthemums and azaleas. One terrace, near the exit, has a complex colourful planting of groundcovers including clover, ivy, climbing Boston ivy and pink evening primroses and is a magnet for bees and butterflies.

However, as is often the case with temple gardens, the main interest is in the walkways leading to the main temple and to and between the various satellite hermitages. The main walk is alongside the Gayacheon stream and passes through regal stands of Korean red pines, and three symbolic gates. Visitors also pass a still pond that reflects the trees surrounding it and contains a stone tortoise sculpture, and a flower meadow containing memorial stellae to several respected monks who studied and taught at Haeinsa in previous centuries.

Further on to the right is a dead tree stump, its roots almost overwhelmed by heaps of votive pebbles. Before it died in 1945, this elm tree was at least one thousand years old and believed to have been planted by the Silla King Aejang in the ninth century when he visited and endowed the temple. Its antiquity and the royal association, leads to even the dead trunk being revered and no attempt has been made to remove it from the otherwise well-tended forest in many decades since its demise. Behind the main temple is another ancient tree with semi-mythic associations. Known as the Haksadae fir tree, it is believed to have grown from the wooden staff of the famous scholar Choi Chi-won who stuck it in the ground here as he retreated to the mountain to a life of contemplation more than 1000 years ago.

Silla King Aejang's elm tree. Many decades after its death, pilgrims still add votive pebbles around its 1000-year-old trunk. © Jill Matthews

141

A visit to Haeinsa is greatly enjoyable for two reasons in addition to experiencing its garden. To see the Tripitaka Koreana is fascinating and if you can time your visit to coincide with one of the daily drumming and chanting rituals which have accompanied the opening and closing of the temple for ten centuries, your Haeinsa cultural immersion experience will be complete.

04   Confucian Literati Gardens

Introduction

The cultural practice of retiring to the countryside and building beautiful contemplative gardens was customary well before the full establishment of Confucianism and Neo-Confucianism during the Joseon dynasty. Many of the surviving Buddhist temple gardens predate the general movement to create Confucian literati gardens, which intensified from the early 1400s onwards. In both the Buddhist and Confucian gardening traditions the careful choice of site according to *pungsu* geomantic principles, led to gardens which maximised the use of borrowed landscape such as mountains and water views. It also led to the creation of sustainable gardens: protective hills or mountains, permanent water supply and plants chosen appropriate to the climate, undoubtedly meant that more of these gardens survived for centuries, despite periods of political turmoil and lack of resources for proper maintenance or reconstruction. Both traditions owe much to the earlier sylvan, even animistic cultural practices of the Korean ancestors. The profound reverence for trees and mountains and the reluctance to impose major structural change on the landscape by earth-moving and redirecting water flows are shared by both traditions.

Nevertheless the Confucian literati gardens differ from the Buddhist temple gardens in many respects. The most obvious reasons are intrusion of the concepts of symmetry and enclosure and a marked concern for relative levels in garden elements, especially in the gardens of Confucian academic institutions and palaces. While Confucian gardens still value the borrowed landscape, they frequently view it from inside an enclosing wall and the actual gardens are designed to be enjoyed by looking within. Buildings surround the garden which is itself seen as an aid to contemplation and an encouragement of seclusion. Commonly Confucian gardens are aligned along a central axis with buildings disposed along it raised to different levels depending on their symbolic importance. Thus the throne hall is the highest building in a palace garden, the study of the teacher is higher than the rooms of his scholars in an educational institution and so on.

There are two main types of Confucian literati gardens, those surrounding educational institutions known as *seowon*, such as the famous **Dosan Seowon** in Andong, and those of private literary figures such as the much admired scholarly retreat gardens **Seoseokji** in Yeongyang county, **Buyongdong** on Bogildo island and **Soswaewon** in Damyang. Both types were instituted by Confucian scholars, who often chose to leave Seoul and its court intrigues behind, in order to pursue lives of quiet study, Confucian rectitude and humility. Generally the private scholarly retreat gardens are less formal in their structure than *seowon* gardens and resemble the earlier Buddhist gardens more.

Dosan Seowon Confucian Academy Garden

Name: Confucian Academy Garden at Dosan 도산서원

Location: 154, Dosanseowon-gil, Dosan-myeon, Andong-si, Gyeongsangbukdo
경상북도 안동시 도산면 도산서원길 154

Best Time to Visit: Late Winter and early Spring for the plum blossoms, late Spring for the peonies or Autumn for the vivid foliage in the surrounding woods.

Of all the Confucian scholar garden-makers whose names we know, Yi Hwang, better known by his pen name Toegye, is certainly the most influential. He was one of the most famous Confucian scholars of the Joseon era, who taught at Sungkyunkwan in Seoul, Korea's oldest university. Until recently his portrait

The famous Confucian scholar Toegye, founder of Dosan Seowon and his beloved plum blossoms on the 1000 won note. Dosan Seowon itself appears on the reverse.© The Bank of Korea

appeared on the front of the Korean 1000 won note and the Confucian academy, Dosan Seowon, which he founded, appeared on its reverse side.

Water in a small well reflects plum leaves. Perhaps Toegye and his students watered the garden from this source.
© Jill Matthews

Despite being repeatedly summoned back to Court and offered several high administrative posts, Toegye's heart remained in the beautiful Dosan countryside where, during the 1560s and 1570s he established a small school for the education of young Confucian gentlemen, which eventually grew into Dosan Seowon. Here he studied, wrote books and poetry, taught for three decades and here he built his ideal garden. He died here and his followers built a shrine here to contain his spirit tablet at which memorial rituals in his honour are still held twice a year. So many students came to study with Toegye

Peonies and Toegye's beloved plum trees line the main axis at Dosan Seowon. © Jill Matthews

One of the simple pavilions along the river bank at Dosan Seowon, this one set in a thicket of Korean red pine and named in Chinese calligraphy carved into a marker rock.
© Jill Matthews

The small lotus pond outside Toegye's study with a Chinese juniper and Chinese calligraphy.
© Jill Matthews

The rectangular pond beside the main Dosan Seowon complex containing many symbolic rocks.
© Jill Matthews

This man-made hill across the river from the main seowon complex is the site of Confucian examinations and a shrine to honour Toegye. © KTO

that his followers greatly expanded his original school and it soon received royal patronage. Many of his students went on to build their own gardens and to write their own garden poetry, so his influence on traditional Korean garden design has been profound. Seoseokji and Choganjeong scholarly retreat gardens, described later, are two examples of gardens built by his pupils and it is easy to see in these gardens the influence of the older garden at Dosan Seowon.

Today the main entrance is approached obliquely through a small Korean red pine forest often used as the setting for historic films. The former approach with its dramatic natural scenery was destroyed by the construction of the Andong dam. The main buildings and garden are sited high enough to command a view through old ginkgo and pine trees over the river to the associated scattered meditation pavilions and the examination hall built to honour Toegye on a distant constructed hill. Within the compound, great attention is paid to the symbolism of the relative levels of each building. For example the library building which held Toegye's own books and those formerly owned personally by Korean kings, is built on a slightly higher level than the main library building. The building which holds Toegye's spirit tablet is on the highest level of all and the students' dormitory is lower than all of these other structures. In this most Confucian of institutions, buildings are all constructed along a strong axis, softened only a little by lines of tree peonies. Nevertheless this strongly geometric, and hierarchical layout, does not constrict. Rather it encourages visitors to look out at the outer garden, surrounding woodland, river and borrowed landscape, to be aware of and to appreciate nature. Outside the walls is a large pond with symbolic rocks, lilies and lotus and an adjacent restored village built initially to house visiting poor but virtuous scholars known as *seonbi*.

Within the walls there are many *Prunus mume* trees. In English the name for these trees is translated variously as Plum or Apricot or Japanese

1   Shrine (Sangdeoksa)
2   Libations hall and ritual implements store (Jeonsacheong)
3   Spirit gate (Naesammun)
4   Lecture hall (Jeongyodang)
5   Upper stewards' house (Sanggojiksa)
6   Western dormitory (Seojae)
7   Eastern dormitory (Dongjae)
8   Storehouse for printing blocks (Jangpangak)
9   Main gate to the academy (Jindomun)
10   West library (Seogwangmyeongsil)
11   East library (Donggwangmyeongsil)
12   Lower stewards' house (Hagojiksa)
13   Dosan private school (Dosan seodang)
14   Student dormitory (Nongunjeongsa)
15   Student dormitory (Yeongnakseojae)

Map of Dosan Seowon

flowering apricot. (A similar confusion exists concerning the name for the trees planted around Confucius' tomb in China.) Representations of their five petalled fragile white blossoms are painted on the ridge poles of several of the buildings within the *seowon*. Whatever their English name, there is no doubt that Toegye loved them. He wrote more than 100 poems, which refer to the attributes of the blossom and, with his dying words, he exhorted his disciples to remember to water the plum trees. In his garden are many other plants with symbolic attributes, including lotus, which grow in a small pond close to the lecture hall, magenta coloured peonies, chrysanthemums, bamboo, junipers, crepe myrtles, maples, magnolias and persimmons. Despite the existence of walls surrounding the main compound much planting exists outside them and the garden shades off gradually into the surrounding woodland in the older Korean gardening tradition seen more commonly in Buddhist temple gardens. In autumn this outer garden is alive with richly coloured maple and ginkgo trees. Originally Toegye also had a terrace constructed in this outer garden, since mostly washed away by floods, which he planted with the 'four gracious friends,' pine tree, bamboo, plum, chrysanthemum and about which he also wrote many poems and essays. Such was the influence of his garden that his disciples included such plants and 'four friends' terraces in their own gardens. A surviving example of such a terrace can be seen in Seoseokji garden described below.

Interestingly, most of the trees and plants in this garden are allowed to reach their full potential with little pruning or unnatural shaping, however the exceptions are the trees and shrubs on the upper level surrounding the shrine and memorial ritual buildings relating to Toegye's spirit tablet. Only here, are trees cloud-pruned and shrubs neatly clipped into geometric mounds. Given his reverence for the natural world and his wish to disturb it as little as possible perhaps Toegye would look askance at such an intrusive form of horticulture practised in his honour.

Soswaewon Scholarly Retreat Garden

Name: Soswaewon (Garden Cleaned by a Fast-Flowing Stream) 소쇄원

Location: 17, Soswaewon-gil, Nam-myeon, Damyang-gun, Jeollanamdo 전라남도 담양군 남면 소쇄원길 17

Soswaewon is probably the most visited of all the scholarly retreat gardens. Its simple structures and naturalistic layout belie an elaborate game of metaphor and literary allusion expressed in the calligraphy and choice of planting. © KTO

Soswaewon garden is probably the most celebrated and visited garden in Korea. It is certainly one of the three most important Confucian scholarly retreat gardens to have survived to the present. The others are: Seoseokji and Buyongdong both described later, however Soswaewon pre-dates these by at least 100 years. It was built by Yang San-bo, (pen name Soswae-ong), in the two decades following his expulsion from Seoul in 1519 during the vicious Literati Purge. Sickened by the loss of his revered teacher, Cho Gwang-jo, whom the victorious court faction forced to commit suicide by drinking poison, he abandoned a promising career in the Joseon court, returned to his home village, and spent the remaining 58 years of his life building and enjoying this garden. Like so many others, this garden was partially destroyed by the Japanese in 1597, but was soon rebuilt by the descendants of Yang San-bo who still maintain the garden today.

The sound of rushing water invites repose in the first pavilion as visitors enter Soswaewon.
© Jill Matthews

Soswaewon, which literally means a 'garden cleaned by a fast-flowing stream,' is built along a fast-flowing stream, which has been only slightly modified to create a small waterfall and a slower reach. It sits on three rustic stone terraces and is partially fenced with walls of stone embedded in terra-cotta coloured clay. At the back there is no wall and the garden shades off into the surrounding forest and farmland. There are three buildings within the garden. The highest and main building *Jewoldang* (Clear Moon Hall) was a private home and study for Yang San-bo; *Gwangpunggak* (Refreshing Breeze Pavilion) beside the flowing stream, was where he entertained guests, and the thatched, *Daebongdae* (Pavilion for Awaiting the Phoenix), greets visitors at the end of the magnificent bamboo-lined entrance pathway. Other named features in the garden include: *Aeyangdan* (Yard for Enjoying Sunshine), the Terrace of Immortality Peach Trees and the *Ogokmun* (Gate of Five Twists and Turns).

The names of each of these buildings and garden features and many of the trees and plants have complex metaphoric and literary significance. Perhaps surprisingly, in the garden of a Confucian scholar, many of these references are to Daoist concepts. For example the Pavilion for Awaiting the Phoenix, is conveniently close to lots of bamboo (*Phyllostachys spp.*) and a couple of Empress trees (*Paulownia tomentosa*). Visitors schooled in Chinese calligraphy and mythology would immediately realise the significance these plantings: bamboo is reputedly the favourite food of the phoenix, and Chinese parasol trees, the favourite roosting place of these mythical creatures. Thus the whole garden can be read as a metaphor for Daoist ideas concerning the quest for immortality. We know from old paintings that there used to be an extensive orchard of Peach trees, which are another symbol for immortality in Daoist literature and art. It is said that Yang San-bo conceived of the whole garden as a material recreation of the realm of the immortals.

Nevertheless because Yang San-bo was a Confucian scholar, he also planted many plants and trees, which are common Confucian symbols. For example bamboo is used as a metaphor for uprightness, strength and resilience because it may bow before a storm but rises again unbroken. Its hollow stems are said to indicate open-mindedness. He planted lotus, in a small pond to signify purity in murky circumstances and the achievement of enlightenment. There are also several plum trees in the garden, which because they bloom in late winter, are a metaphor for virtuous character borne of rigorous self-examination. Then

153

there is the Yard for Enjoying Sunshine, which actually is the warmest part of the garden where the snow melts first, creating an *um-yang* contrast with the surrounding snow and shade, and can be seen as a symbol of the attainment of reward by tenacious application. In spring it becomes a lovely wildflower meadow, a common feature of many different types of Korean gardens.

Soswaewon was the inspiration for numerous poems both by its owner and his friends. Some of these are written on plaques hanging in the Refreshing Breeze Pavilion. Among the most famous are the 48 poems by Gim In-hu, including one dedicated to the Gate of Five Twists and Turns:

> *Sitting near a babbling brook flowing into a nearby pond*
> *Hearing it wind through its five twists and turns*
> *I want to sit under the apricot tree*
> *And contemplate nature the way Confucius did*
> *When he too once sat beside a stream.*

This poem is both a reference to a much older Chinese poem concerning the many bends in the stream of life and to the belief that Confucius lectured on a podium made of apricot (or possibly ginkgo) wood. Hence ginkgoes and apricots are planted frequently in Confucian scholarly gardens. Both are present in Soswaewon.

Clear Moon Hall and Refreshing Breeze Pavilion both refer to the biography of Zhou Dunyi, a Chinese philosopher whom Yang San-bo particularly admired. In it the biographer said:

> *Spending time with him was as refreshing as feeling a cool breeze on your skin while looking at the clear moon in the sky after the rain has stopped.*

Simple, rustic materials used throughout Soswaewon emphasised the humility and lack of ostentation of Yang San-bo.

At first view Soswaewon seems to be a simple, almost rustic, garden containing humble buildings, however despite its simple appearance it is loaded with philosophic and literary meaning. It can be understood on many levels in addition to the purely aesthetic and horticultural.

Buyongdong Scholarly Retreat Garden

Name: Buyongdong (Grotto of Half Bloomed lotus Flower) 부용동

Location: 57, Buhwang-gil, Bogil-myeon, Wando-gun, Jeollanamdo 전라남도 완도군 보길면 부황길 57

Best time to visit: March when the camellias bloom.

Buyongdong garden was made by Yun Seon-do, better known by his pen name Gosan. It is on an island off the south-western tip of Korea and slow to reach by ferry but well worth the visit. Gosan was a senior civil official and poet of the mid-Joseon period who retired from Court after experiencing the humiliation of seeing his King, Injo, surrender and kneel to the Chinese Qing Emperor Taizong. Thereupon he renounced the world and retreated to Bogildo island at the southernmost tip of the Korean peninsula where, starting in 1637, he built the garden and lived a very sociable but virtuous life for another 30 years until he died at age 85.

Here he wrote one of the most famous poems of classical Korean literature—The Fisherman's Calendar (*Eobu sasisa*). It is significant because it was not written in classical Chinese like most Korean literature of the period, but rather in vernacular Korean. It can be regarded as a sustained metaphor for his own life-that of a wise man who has turned his back on the world and lived in harmony with nature, and in accord with his personal principles, thereby attaining wisdom and virtue. In addition to writing poetry in his

The island in front of Seyeonjeong pavilion in the heart of Buyongdong formed a stage for many cultural performances. © Jill Matthews

Despite the general reluctance of Korean garden designers to make massive changes to the topography of garden sites, they sometimes took measures to slow the natural flow of water and allow for reflections of garden features. © Jill Matthews

garden, Gosan studied and taught Confucian classics, and entertained fellow literati at drinking and poetry parties. Few days went by without lavish music, dance events or archery competitions. There are several performance platforms scattered about the garden, including one on an island in the pond in front of Seyeonjeong pavilion where child musicians in vivid costumes used to dance and play instruments or row about singing.

The main garden is extensive but not enclosed by walls. To one side it is bounded by market gardens. On the other it blends into forest and mountainside where Gosan built several viewing pavilions for energetic climbers.

There are many old trees in this garden including Korean red pines, a symbol of loyalty and fidelity, a large grove of ancient camellias, called 'the friend of scholars,' junipers, willows, persimmons and rhododendrons. In addition to the lotus and water lilies often are found in Korean gardens, a diversity of smaller water plants thrive in the pond and slower reaches of the stream. The pond behind Seyeonjeong pavilion contains numerous rocks, which, while local, have clearly been arranged for aesthetic effect and to direct the stream waters somewhat. Many were given specific metaphoric names such as 'crouching dragon' and 'toad about to leap,' which refer to particular events in Chinese mythology and literature. Thus, as in so many Korean gardens, in this one there is a deep level of literary symbolism, which would have been appreciated by visiting well-versed literati friends in addition to its purely aesthetic pleasures.

Gosan's 'Song of My Five Friends' (*Owuga*) was written in the garden. It is a common literary tradition, to nominate 'five friends' and it is easy to see why Gosan, writing in this beautiful garden, chose water, stone, pine, bamboo and moon as his best friends.

Without disturbing nature too much, the rocks in Buyongdong pond have been subtly rearranged and named to enhance the literary games played by Gosan and his guests. © Jill Matthews

Toad About to Leap rock in Buyongdong. © Jill Matthews

Seongyojang Country Estate Garden

Name: Seongyojang (Boat-Bridge Hamlet) 선교장

Location: 63, Unjeong-gil, Gangneung-si, Gangwondo 강원도 강릉시 운정길 63

Best time to visit: Summer when the lotus are in bloom, however the crepe myrtles are beautiful in most seasons.

Seongyojang is one of the most intact aristocratic country estates in South Korea. Lee Nae-beon (1703-1781) the eleventh generation descendant of Prince

The surviving traditional buildings sit harmoniously within the Seongyojang garden. © KTO

The plantings at Seongyojang are much simplified, however many original features such the well, the iris bed, the small lily pond, and the strolling and vegetable gardens remain. © Jill Matthews

Hyoryeong commenced construction of the manor and gardens around 1756. These were extended and improved by several of the 10 generations of descendants who have lived here for over 300 years. The family continues to live in a modern annex on the hill to the right as you enter. Officially such an aristocratic family would only have been entitled to build a home of 99 *kan*[*] but in fact the buildings total 130 *kan* so the family must have wielded considerable wealth and influence over a long period.

The syllable *seon* in the name means 'boat' because originally the estate was approached by boat over the nearby Lake Gyeongpo. Seongyojang means 'boat-bridge hamlet.' Nowadays the lake is much reduced in circumference and a road and fringe of ugly modern buildings intervene between the estate and its formerly beautiful view, however in many other respects Seongyojang, including its gardens, is well preserved and maintained and the plantings only

* *kan*: a unit of measuring area of korean traditional house, one *kan* ≒ 6.958~8.946ft

In Hwallaejeong pavilion, gentlemen scholars drank tea, composed poetry and enjoyed the changing beauty of the lotus and crepe myrtles in each season. The pavilion appears to float over the lotus pond on its stone pillars. © Jill Matthews

162

The lotus pond at Seongyojang, is square and contains one round island. It is a metaphor for the Daoist idea of the fundamental complementarity of the universe. Such ponds were common in the gardens of Confucian gentlemen. © KTO

a little simplified.

The first thing to notice as you enter is the Hwallaejeong pavilion which floats on four stone pillars cantilevered over its own square, lotus-filled pond. A bridge leads over the lotus to an island on which are planted Korean red pines. The pond is surrounded by crepe myrtle trees, beautiful in all seasons. To the left is a strolling garden full of iris, day lilies and other perennials shaded by conifer shrubs and small fruit trees. It terminates at a small pond now planted with water lilies, though perhaps formerly a well. Behind one line of buildings is a typical flower terrace (*hwagye*) brimming with peonies and other small plants, which emphasise the changing of the seasons. The whole estate is protected by low hills, which, with the lake in front, would have made the site geomantically perfect. Although it seems the plantings on these hills have been much simplified, they are still crowned by a fringe of auspicious Korean red pines.

This is still a productive garden with extensive vegetable and herb plantings and many fruit trees. One of the traditional buildings at the rear is still in use for the making of *kimchi* and the local special variety of *tofu*, which are served at the breakfasts provided for guests.

Many residential courses in Confucian matters are held at Seongyojang so it is not unusual to find traditionally dressed gentlemen wandering through the gardens as they would have

Towards the rear of Seongyojang there are several flower terraces planted with symbolic plants such as peonies. © Jill Matthews

The many flowers in the strolling garden within Seongyojang give aesthetic pleasure in every season. Only the fruit trees are productive. © Jill Matthews

Though much simplified, the plantings on the protective hills surrounding Seongyojang still provide a refreshing walk on a hot afternoon. © KTO

done for the last three hundred years. It is possible to stay in one of the many restored *hanok* (Korean traditional house) style rooms on the estate and so to have the privilege of wandering through the gardens yourself, early in the morning or late in the evening after the day-trippers and wedding photographers have departed. Such an experience gives you a real taste of the calm understated elegance of an upper class private Korean garden.

Ojukheon Country Estate Garden

Name: Ojukheon (Garden of Black Bamboo) 오죽헌

Location: 24, Yulgok-ro, 3139beon-gil, Gangneung-si, Gangwondo 강원도 강릉시 율곡로 3139번길 24

The garden at Ojukheon is also situated on the former edge of Lake Gyeongpo, not far from Seongyojang country estate in Gangneung. Its oldest structures are probably at least 200 years older than those at nearby Seongyojang, having been built during the reign of the eleventh Joseon King Jungjong in the mid-1500s. Ojukheon was the childhood home of Shin Saimdang, the widely revered female artist, calligrapher and scholar. Shin Saimdang had no brothers

The grand entrance to Ojukheon, a garden now regarded as a national treasure and the object of mass tourism. © KTO

and consequently attained an education denied to most high class Confucian women of the time. Much of her calligraphy and many of her delicate, beautiful and botanically accurate paintings of plants and insects, are displayed in the museum at the entrance to the estate and its gardens. It is known that she grew most of the plants featured in her paintings in the garden at Ojukheon during her lifetime, although sadly the plantings in the garden today have been much simplified. Her paintings have appeared on several Korean currency notes and postage stamps.

Shin Saimdang was the mother of the very famous Joseon dynasty statesman and scholar Yi I (pen name Yulgok). She lavished her knowledge and skill on the early education of her son who was a precocious academic achiever, and passed the preliminary civil service exams when he was only 13 while also studying Daoism and Buddhism in addition to the Confucian classics and Chinese literature. After winning the first place in the State exam in 1564, he visited Toegye at Dosan Seowon where it is said they conversed non-stop for three whole days. While there he no doubt observed and was influenced by its beautiful garden. As a social reformer and statesman, Yulgok warned repeatedly of the need to prepare for invasion by the Japanese and when his warnings were

Ojukheon was the childhood home and garden of Shin Saimdang. Here she educated her famous statesman son Yulgok and made her botanical paintings.
© Jill Matthews

ignored at court he returned to his beloved country estate Ojukheon. Sadly his warnings proved to be only too accurate when General Hideyoshi invaded in 1592, and the Imjin Wars began eight years after his death.

Like his mother, Yulgok was a keen gardener and has also appeared on more than one banknote. On the 5,000 won note, the background to his portrait is the main pavilion at Ojukheon and the black bamboo, which gives the garden its name. One of his mother's plant paintings decorates the back.

The very filial descendants of these two eminent Koreans continue to maintain their ancestral home and gardens and several buildings display original artefacts relating to both mother and son. Many Koreans, including scholars, students and Presidents, regard Ojukheon as a shrine and visit in their thousands as a sign of respect and to learn more of their history. It is

율곡이이

Yulgok retired from Court to Ojukheon when his warnings of imminent Japanese invasion were ignored. © Jill Matthews

Behind the portrait of Yulgok is the black bamboo after which Ojukheon is named. On the reverse is a painting by his mother Shin Saimdang. © The Bank of Korea

Dancheong painting with many horticultural symbols adorn the structures within Ojukheon and here frame stands of black bamboo which have grown in Okjukheon since the time of Shin Saimdang and Yulgok. © Jill Matthews

Chochungdo (grass and insects) is one of Shin Saimdang's famous paintings. © National Museum of Korea

therefore a very busy place and the approaches are landscaped in a modern style and contain large statues of both Shin Saimdang, and her son Yulgok, souvenir shops, restaurants and car and bus parks.

The gardens have necessarily been modified to cope with such mass tourism and can almost never be enjoyed in silence or solitude. However once inside the estate enclosure it is still possible to admire the screens of Chinese black bamboo (*Phyllostachys nigra* 'Munro') and the towering stands of Korean red pine beyond the compound walls. Within the enclosure there are several significant trees including persimmon, pomegranate, crepe myrtle, plum,

Magnolia, azaleas and maples in a quiet corner of Ojukheon. © KTO

magnolia and juniper. Many smaller plants familiar from old Chinese gardens are also present including peonies, hostas, hydrangeas and flowering Chinese quince.

Choganjeong Scholarly Retreat Garden

Name: Choganjeong (Studying at a Bend in a Stream Pavilion) 초간정
Location: 874, Yongmungyeongcheon-ro, Yongmun-myeon, Yecheon-gun, Gyeong-sangbukdo 경상북도 예천군 용문면 용문경천로 874

This woodland garden was built in 1582, by Gwon Mun-hae (pen name Chogan), an official in the court of King Seonjo. Chogan was yet another student of

Toegye who built the famous Dosan *seowon* garden. Thus he was well versed in Confucian and Daoist ideas as well as garden design. Like many such scholars Chogan retired from the politics and conflicts of court life relatively early, seeking a reclusive life amidst nature. Back in his home village, Jukrim-ri, he built the garden usually called by the name of its main pavilion *Choganjeong*, which means 'Studying at a Bend in a Stream.' The pavilion is small and rustic and is an excellent example of the Korean curved roofline, so distinctive when compared with garden structures in Chinese or Japanese gardens. It is certainly

Choganjeong pavilion in which Gwon Mun-hae compiled his famous Encyclopaedia of Korean Writings. © Jill Matthews

the heart of the garden, however the whole garden extends over 15 acres, not separated from the surrounding countryside by any walls, and is more correctly referred to as *Wonrim* or 'nature garden.' Beautifully sited both aesthetically and geomantically, it stretches along the banks of a clear mountain stream which pivots abruptly at a pool edged by many strangely shaped rocks immediately below the pavilion. It contains many mature Korean red pines, oaks, willows and elms and a lush cultivated wildflower meadow replete with wild asters, coreopsis, hardy chrysanthemums and many beautiful wild grasses in their season. The sound of the stream water cascading over the rocks, which inspired Chogan to write his garden poetry five hundred years ago, is just as enjoyable today. It is a lovely place to eat a picnic and calm your mind and you are likely to be the only person there. Chogan described his garden in a short poem:

Under the blue sky,
A valley surrounds this place
Like a folding screen
While water gently waves.

In this lovely space he settled down to complete his life's project, a great literary work, the Encyclopaedia of Korean Writings Arranged by Rhyme (*Daedong unbu gunok*). This 20 volume work is a collection of rhyming couplets and

Chogan could hear the sound of the stream as it flowed over rough rocks below and pivoted around the base of his rustic study. His name for this pavilion 'Studying at the Bend of a Stream' is both a reference to a Chinese poem and a statement of fact and has become the name for his entire garden.
© Jill Matthews

aphorisms arranged by topics such as — geography, names of kingdoms, family names and lineages, filial sons, chaste women, official titles, immortals, pen names, names of flowers and animals and so forth. Inspired by a dictionary of rhyming phrases, written by a Chinese scholar of the Yuan dynasty around

An example of the woodblock pages of the Encyclopaedia of Korean Writings, still preserved by the descendants of Gwon Mun-hae 500 years after its creation.
© Yecheon County Office

1270, Chogan's work was a distillation of centuries of earlier Korean literature and covered every Korean dynasty from the mythical founder Dangun up to his own day in the early Joseon era. This scholar was a near contemporary of Shakespeare, yet he was accessing and systematising a literary tradition, which already stretched back at least two millennia. What a resource for aristocratic Koreans searching for a perfect name for a garden or pavilion, or inspiration for garden poetry!

Another astonishing thing about his *Daedong unbu gunok* was that it was not published until two hundred years after his death. In 1798, Gwon's seventh generation lineal descendent published it, printed from woodblocks still retained in Jukrim-ri by the current head of his lineage. Chogan's descendants have twice rebuilt the Choganjeong pavilion after its destruction by invading Japanese and Chinese armies. The continued preservation and restoration of both garden and encyclopaedia is an example without parallel of steadfast filial dedication and literary continuity, not to mention the crucial role of Korea's historic clans (*jongga*) in the preservation of traditional Korean gardens.

Imdaejeong Wonrim Woodland Garden

Name: Imdaejeong (Watching Mountain Pavilion) 임대정
Location: 48, Sangsa 1-gil, Nam-myeon, Hwasun-gun, Jeollanamdo 전라남도 화순군 남면 상사1길 48
Best time to visit: Summer when both the lotus and the crepe myrtles are in bloom or late winter and early spring when the cherry trees blossom.

There has been a woodland garden on this site since the late-1500s. The original owner was Nam Eon-gi, (pen name Goban) whose garden encompassed a small Confucian *seowon*. However the main pavilion, which now stands on the highest point of the garden, was first built in 1862 by Min Ju-hyeon (pen name Sa-ae) who was the deputy minister of military affairs during the reign of Joseon King Cheoljong. When he retired from Court, this garden became his life's focus and he added many Daoist, even Shamanistic elements into it.

Sa-ae called his garden Imdaejeong which is a reference to a Chinese Song dynasty poem by Zhou Dunyi, entitled 'Sitting by a Riverside, Thinking of a Mountain' or alternatively 'To Watch the Mountain at the Water's Edge.' The garden is protected from behind, by a range of low hills. There is a view from the pavilion to Mt. Bongjeongsan, the setting sun, and the cultivated fields below the lower garden ponds. These ponds are fed by Sapyeongcheon stream which flows from the west through the garden to the north-east. The garden therefore possesses four of the most important attributes of traditional Korean gardens: excellent geomantic properties; spectacular use of borrowed landscape; perfect site selection for sustainable gardening including a permanent natural water supply; and it is itself a physical manifestation of an important piece of classical Chinese literature.

The upper pond next to the pavilion used to be fed by a diverted stream.

Three islands survive in the lower ponds. Originally each island had either three rocks or three trees or both, on them. © Jill Matthews

Water flowed through it to the lower ponds via a rock arrangement, making a picturesque waterfall. Sadly these days the upper pond is dry and the waterfall is no more, but its little central island still retains its rock inscribed with Chinese calligraphy meaning 'fragrance pond', 'purity pond', and 'purifying mind'. The pavilion is still surrounded by a strolling garden with black bamboo, red spider lilies, prostrate junipers, oak, elm, Korean red pine, maple, ginkgo and rhus trees. The pavilion retains an elegant name-plate and several Chinese character poetry boards within.

The uppermost pond in Imdaejeong is dry these days but retains its symbolic rocks and island and Chinese calligraphy. © Jill Matthews

An old Chinese juniper embraces a rock on the edge of the pond in the upper garden. The calligraphy means 'purity pond' or 'fragrance pond' or 'purifying mind.' © Jill Matthews

There are two larger ponds in the lower garden, one square and planted with pink lotus, and one sickle shape and planted with white ones. Between them the ponds contain three islands, three significant shapely rocks and trees planted on the islands in threes. This insistent use of trinities is also a common feature of traditional Korean gardens and may bear different meanings depending on the garden. Here it is believed to represent heaven, earth and man, the *um-yang* philosophy and Daoism. The lower ponds are fringed with willow, cherry trees and crepe myrtle, which, together with the diversity of trees on the upper level of the garden, provide colour and interest for most times of the year.

One of the lower ponds is planted with pink flowered lotus, the other with the rarer white. ©Jill Matthews

Seoseokji Scholarly Retreat Garden

Name: Seoseokji (Auspicious Rock Pond) 서석지

Location: 10, Seoseokji 1-gil, Ibam-myeon, Yeongyang-gun, Gyeongsangbukdo
경상북도 영양군 입암면 서석지1길 10

Best time to visit: July when the lotus blooms.

Seoseokji is considered to be one of the three most perfect Confucian gardens in Korea. It is a small elegant gem, at its most beautiful in July, when the lotus blooms. This garden was first built in 1613, the year of Shakespeare's death in England, by Jeong Yeong-bang (pen name Seokmun), a highly qualified Neo-Confucian scholar who had studied under the even more famous Toegye, builder of the earlier influential Dosan Seowon garden. Although qualified to be a government officer in the Joseon dynasty court, Seokmun retired from Seoul and spent his life here in his garden, reading in his library, writing poetry

Seoseokji is small but elegant, designed with the eye of an artist. © Jill Matthews

Every one of the 90 rocks in the Seoseokji pond is named for some attribute or literary reference.

and thinking. Originally the garden was much more extensive and it was easier to see the geomantic perfection of the site, however today only the inner garden remains. This walled garden is attached to a residence, and contains a library *Juiljae* (Concentrating on One Thing) and a garden pavilion *Gyeongjeong* (Mindfullness). Its central feature is a square lotus pond from which the whole garden takes its name: 'auspicious rock pond.' In addition to its numerous lotus plants, the pond contains an archipelago of 60 visible rocks and at least 30 submerged rocks. Seokmun named every one of these rocks, not for any physical resemblance they may have—there is no 'turtle rock' which looks like a turtle—but rather each rock name refers to a Confucian teaching, a quote from the works of Mencius, a Chinese work of literature or a Daoist aphorism.

An example of a Confucian reference is the rock named *Tagyeongban* literally 'place for cleaning of the hat strings' which is a reference to a poem from the Chinese Zhou dynasty, entitled 'The Fisherman,' which is itself a metaphor for 'serving in office when the time is right but living in seclusion at times of chaos and disorder.' Interestingly, unlike most of the other rocks in the pond, this particular rock is occasionally fully submerged, much like a scholar who withdraws from court during difficult times. An example of a rock with Daoist significance is *Huijeob*, literally 'enjoying being a butterfly rock,' which refers to the Chinese Butterfly Dream story in which a man taking a nap, dreams he is a butterfly and when he awakes is uncertain whether he is a butterfly dreaming he is a man, or a man who dreamt he was a butterfly. This is a neat metaphor for the Daoist aim of transcending and forgetting oneself. Almost all the rocks in the pond have such multi-layered meanings, and in Seokmun's time would have served as tools for meditation or stimuli for literary creation.

Set into the pond is an elevated terrace with a rock bearing the Chinese characters for *saudan*—A Platform for Four Old Friends. There, Seokmun wrote the following poem:

> *Plum and chrysanthemum stand out in a snow-covered landscape*
> *Pine and bamboo give nature colour after frost*
> *With pine, bamboo, plum and chrysanthemum as my friends in winter*
> *I will have companions as long as I live.*

These 'four friends'—plum, chrysanthemum, bamboo and pine—continue to grow on the Saudan in his garden three hundred years later and, because they remain green or even blossom during cold times, should together be understood to symbolise steadfastness and perseverance in times of adversity.

Seokmun was not the first man of letters to group these plants together

Seokseokji Platform (Saudan) for Four Old Friends still planted with plum, chrysanthemum, bamboo and pine 400 years after Seokmun wrote his poem. © Jill Matthews

because of what they symbolise: many earlier Chinese and Korean poems and paintings had done so. Because of their common literary and artistic heritage, Korean gardens share many such symbolic plants with Chinese gardens.. Both Korean and Chinese poetry contain many references to plum blossom, chrysanthemums, pine and bamboo, and also to juniper trees, lotus, ginkgo, peonies and orchids, almost all of which grow in Seosoekji garden. Gardens containing them should be considered as embodiments of the virtues long associated with them.

In addition to the 'four friends,' the garden contains a magnificent ginkgo tree, understood as a symbol of Confucian dedication to learning.

Ginkgo trees are commonly planted at the entrances of Korean gardens and are a sign of Confucian associations. Seokmun, a renowned Confucian scholar, followed this tradition when he planted this ginkgo at Seoseokji. © KTO

Every plant in Seoseokji, including this species rose, is chosen for its simplicity of form. © Jill Matthews

Altogether the garden is an elegant, harmonious and peaceful place, with rocks, trees and plants carefully arranged to epitomise the desire of Seokmun and his friends to lead lives of contemplative freedom secluded from worldly attachments and distractions.

Gwanghalluwon Garden

Name: Gwanghalluwon (initially known as Gwangtongnu) 광한루원

Location: 1447, Yocheon-ro, Namwon-si, Jeollabukdo 전라북도 남원시 요천로 1447

Gwanghalluwon garden is almost 600 years old. It was first created in 1419 during the reign of the famous Joseon King, Sejong. Many changes have occurred during its centuries of existence although fragments of the original design remain. Originally the garden was intended as a symbolic recreation of the land of the immortals, an idea often represented in earlier Chinese gardens. Thus the centerpiece is a pond containing three islands, named

Gwanghallu pavilion and the Ojakgyo bridge (Magpie Bridge) are the central features of Gwanghalluwon. © KNA

Penglai, Fangzang and Yingzhou, (or Bongrae, Bangjang and Youngju in Korean) and planted in the Chinese manner, intended as metaphoric homes for the immortals. The garden contains many stone carvings of tortoises and hares, reputed to guide seekers to the realm of the immortals and to the mythical Dragon Palace beneath the sea.

Despite its original Chinese concept, later additions incorporate many references to Korean folk tales and mythology. The principal pavilion, Gwanghallu, which gives the garden its present name, is a reference to the Moon Palace of Korean mythology. Like many others it was burnt down during the Japanese invasion in 1597, but rebuilt in the seventeenth century. The Ojakgyo bridge (Magpie Bridge) which leads to the pavilion, was built in the fifteenth century and refers to a famous Korean folk tale concerning star-

Gwanghalluwon has many symbolic and figurative stones because of the Chinese influence on its early design. © KTO

crossed lovers separated by the milky way and only able to meet once a year on a bridge made by a flock of magpies. The Chunhyang (Fragrance of spring) Shrine is dedicated to another pair of fictional star-crossed lovers but has a happy ending. One day in May, a young man saw Chunhyang, a beautiful girl, swinging in Gwanghalluwon and instantly fell in love with her and she with him. However his family did not approve because she was the daughter of a courtesan. They took him to Seoul to prepare for the State exam and forget her. Nevertheless she remained steadfast in her affection for him in his absence despite many enticing offers from more powerful men. Eventually he returned secretly, risking imprisonment, and they were united. The story is regarded as a celebration of fidelity and of the over-coming of social barriers, by the common people.

The garden is beautiful in all sea-sons with bare branches and snow-etched pavilions reflected in the water in winter, azaleas and magnolias in bloom in spring, crepe myrtles, lotus and water lilies in summer, and glorious autumnal colour on the ginkgoes and other deciduous trees.

Gwanghalluwon is the central ven-ue for the annual Namwon Chunhyang Festival, one of the oldest in Korea, each May. During this month the garden hosts multiple cultural events and performanc-es, many emphasizing the star-crossed lovers associations described above. Visi-tor numbers at this time may impede quiet

One of the glories of this old garden are its many ancient trees. © KNA

enjoyment of its gardens, although many will also regard the traditional cultural aspects of the festival as an enhancement to their visits.

Mugiyeondang Pond and Pavilion Garden

Name: Mugiyeondang (Lotus Pond Garden at Mugi) 무기연당

Location: 33, Mugi 1-gil, Chilwon-eup, Haman-gun, Gyeongsangnamdo 경상남도 함안군 칠원읍 무기1길 33

Further Information: On application to the house next to Mugiyeondang a member of the Yu clan will unlock the painted gateway to enable short visits by the public.

Mugiyeondang is a rare example of late Joseon garden design. Situated right next to the main residence of the Yu clan in Mugi Village, it was built to honour an illustrious ancestor of the clan, Ju Jae-seong, known as Master Gukdam, a Neo-Confucian scholar of note. In 1728 when there was an uprising against King Yeongjo, Master Gukdam raised an army of volunteers, provisioned them at his own expense, and fought bravely with them in support of the King. Consequently the pond, and one of the three pavilions surrounding it, were constructed by soldiers of the King to honour his loyalty and assistance. For a time the site housed Giyang *seowon*, but like many small private academies, this was ordered to be demolished during the later reign of King Gojong. The Yu family continues to maintain the garden and added a new shrine pavilion as recently as 1971.

The garden is small and surrounded by a rectangular stone and rammed earth wall capped with ceramic tiles with one large ceremonial gate with *dancheong* decorations. The basic layout is known to be unchanged since its inception from an old painting called Hahwanjeongdo.

The immediate overall impression of the garden is its austerity. One

何搜亭圖

Hahwanjeongdo. This picture shows how Mugieyeondang might look at that time.
© Haman Museum

Even when the azaleas bloom in Mugiyeondang, the garden is austere, very suitable for a military hero. © Jill Matthews

can imagine that a military man like Master Gukdam would have felt right at home here. The central feature is the rectangular pond with rough stone banks like two-tiered ramparts. In the middle of the pond sits a complicated rectangular island constructed of many stones on different levels and planted with a box-leafed holly bush and various ground covers. This style of artificial stone mountain island is understood to be a Daoist element. The three pavilion buildings are unpainted and have pillar posts some of which deliberately retain the shape of the original tree trunks in an agreeably rustic manner. There is one grand old Korean pine tree which frames the main scholars pavilion and an ancient Chinese juniper, as well as an array of smaller trees and shrubs such as osmanthus, crepe myrtle, rhododendron, camellias, prunus and Japanese maple and cercis. Suprisingly for a garden named after them, there seem to be no lotuses in the pond. Ginkgo and persimmon trees outside the north-eastern wall soften the background to the garden and clearly mark the passage of the seasons.

Stela inscribed in Chinese to commemorate the famous Confucian scholar and loyal soldier. © Jill Matthews

The new pavilion, built recently by filial descendants to honour Master Gukdam, has rustic elements such as the tree-shaped uprights and revealed grain of the timber. © KNA

Part 3

Tables *and* Diagrams

A Directory of Notable Gardens in Korea

Name	Hangeul Name	Address	Hangeul Address	Comment	Further information
Anapji Pond	안압지			See Donggung Palace and Wolji Pond	
Biwon	비원			See Changdeokgung Palace	
Bulguksa Temple	불국사	385, Bulguk-ro, Gyeongju-si, Gyeongsangbukdo	경상북도 경주시 불국로 385	Buddhist temple garden—Surrounds a temple one thousand four hundred years old. See page 128.	http://www.bulguksa.or.kr (in Korean) http://english.visitkorea.or.kr/enu/ATR/SI_EN_3_1_1_1.jsp?cid=264261
Buyongdong	부용동	57, Buhwang-gil, Bogil-myeon, Wando-gun, Jeollanamdo	전라남도 완도군 보길면 부황길 57	Confucian scholarly retreat garden—Nearly five hundred years old. See page 156.	http://korean.visitkorea.or.kr/kor/bz15/where/where_main_search.jsp?cid=126422 (in Korean)
Changdeokgung Palace	창덕궁	99, Yulgok-ro, Jongno-gu, Seoul	서울특별시 종로구 율곡로 99	Palace containing the most intact of Joseon dynasty palace gardens. This garden has many names. It was formerly known as Geumwon (금원, Forbidden) or Huwon (후원, Rear), but now is known as Biwon (비원, Secret garden). About six hundred years old. UNESCO world heritage site. See page 81.	http://eng.cdg.go.kr
Choganjeong Wonrim	초간정 원림	874, Yongmungyeongcheon-ro, Yongmun-myeon, Yecheon-gun, Gyeongsangbukdo	경상북도 예천군 용문면 용문경천로 874	Confucian scholarly retreat garden—In woodland nature garden style. Nearly five hundred years old. See page 170.	https://korean.visitkorea.or.kr/kor/bz15/where/where_tour.jsp?cid=128135 (in Korean)
Chollipo Arboretum	천리포 수목원	187, Cheollipo 1-gil, Sowon-myeon, Taean-gun, Chungcheongnamdo	충청남도 태안군 소원면 천리포1길 187	A modern garden with a world class collection of magnolias and hollies donated to Korea by Ferris Miller.	http://www.chollipo.org/eng
Daereungwon	대릉원	9, Gyerim-ro, Gyeongju-si, Gyeongsangbukdo	경상북도 경주시 계림로 9	Royal tomb park—Final resting place of many unnamed Buddhist members of the Silla dynasty. There are several clusters of tumuli tombs, some excavated, and artifacts displayed in nearby museum. See page 111.	http://english.visitkorea.or.kr/enu/ATR/SI_EN_3_1_1_1.jsp?cid=264117
Donggung Palace and Wolji Pond	동궁과 월지	102, Wonhwa-ro, Gyeongju-si, Gyeongsangbukdo	경상북도 경주시 원화로 102	Palace garden—(formerly known as Imhaejeonji, Anapji). Only surviving Silla dynasty palace garden. Nearly one thousand four hundred years old. Fully restored. See page 95.	https://korean.visitkorea.or.kr/kor/bz15/where/where_main_search.jsp?cid=128526 (in Korean)
Donggureung	동구릉	197, Donggureung-ro, Guri-si, Gyeonggido	경기도 구리시 동구릉로 197	Royal tomb park—Final resting place of 7 kings of Joseon and important members of royal family including the dynasty founder King Taejo. On the outskirts of Seoul. A good day trip. See page 105.	http://english.visitkorea.or.kr/enu/ATR/SI_EN_3_1_1_1.jsp?cid=264360
Dosan Seowon	도산서원	154, Dosanseowon-gil, Dosan-myeon, Andong-si, Gyeongsangbukdo	경상북도 안동시 도산면 도산서원길 154	Confucian Academy garden—Most famous of the seowon gardens and well preserved. Nearly five hundred years old. See page 144.	http://www.dosanseowon.com/english/main.asp

Gwanghalluwon	광한루원	1447, Yocheon-ro, Namwon-si, Jeollabukdo	전라북도 남원시 요천로 1447	Confucian provincial country garden—(also known as Gwangtongnu). Venue for annual Namwon Chunhyang Festival. Six hundred years old. See page 183.	http://english.visitkorea.or.kr/enu/ATR/SI_EN_3_1_1_1.jsp?cid=264601
Gwangtongnu	광통루			See Gwanghalluwon	
Gyeongbokgung Palace	경복궁	161, Sajik-ro, Jongno-gu, ス Seoul	서울특별시 종로구 사직로 161	Palace garden—Surrounds the main Joseon dynasty palace. Main old parts of the garden are Hyangwonjeong, Gyeonghoeru and Amisan. About five hundred years old. Under restoration but well worth a visit. See page 87.	http://www.royalpalace.go.kr:8080/html/eng
Gyeonghoeru	경회루			See Gyeongbokgung Palace	
Haeinsa Temple	해인사	122, Haeinsa-gil, Gaya-myeon, Hapcheon-gun, Gyeongsangnamdo	경상남도 합천군 가야면 해인사길 122	Buddhist temple garden—Surrounds one of the three jewels amongst Korean Buddhist temples, home of the famous Tripitaka Koreana. About Twelve hundred years old. See page 136.	http://koreantemples.com/?p=253 http://english.visitkorea.or.kr/enu/ATR/SI_EN_3_1_1_1.jsp?cid=264238 http://www.haeinsa.or.kr/ (in Korean)
Hee Won Garden	희원	38, Everland-ro 562beon-gil, Pogok-eup, Cheoin-gu, Yongin-si, Gyeonggido	경기도 용인시 처인구 포곡읍 에버랜드로 562번길 38	Garden at Ho-Am Art Museum which houses the art collection of Lee Byung-chul, the founder of the Samsung Group. This is a modern garden but exhibits many of the characteristics of old traditional Korean garden design.	http://hoam.samsungfoundation.org/eng/html/heewon/heewon_index.asp
Ho-Am Art Museum	호암미술관			See Hee Won Garden	
Huwon	후원			See Changdeokgung Palace	
Hyangwonjeong	향원정			See Gyeongbokgung Palace	
Imdaejeong Wonrim	임대정 원림	48, Sangsa 1-gil, Nam-myeon, Hwasun-gun, Jeollanamdo	전라남도 화순군 남면 상사1길 48	Confucian scholarly retreat garden—In woodland nature garden style. More than five hundred years old. See page 174.	http://korean.visitkorea.or.kr/kor/bz15/where/where_main_search.jsp?cid=126978 (in Korean)
Imhaejeonji	임해전지			See Donggung Palace and Wolji Pond	
Mugiyeondang	무기연당	33, Mugi 1-gil, Chilwon-eup, Haman-gun, Gyeongsangnamdo	경상남도 함안군 칠원읍 무기1길 33	Confucian scholarly retreat garden—About three hundred years old. See page 186.	http://tour.haman.go.kr/sub/01/04_03.jsp (in Korean)
Myeongokheon Wonrim	명옥헌 원림	103, Husan-gil, Goseo-myeon, Damyang-gun, Jeollanamdo	전라남도 담양군 고서면 후산길 103	Confucian scholarly retreat garden at least 300 years old.	http://english.visitkorea.or.kr/enu/ATR/SI_EN_3_1_1_1.jsp?cid=1173048
National Museum of Korea	국립 중앙박물관	137, Seobinggo-ro, Yongsan-gu, Seoul	서울특별시 용산구 서빙고로 137	Built on the former American armed forces golf course, to one side of the Museum, this lovely modern garden displays many characteristics of traditional Korean gardens and houses an interesting collection of ancient sculpture and architectural remnants.	http://www.museum.go.kr/site/eng/home

193

Ojukheon	오죽헌	24, Yulgok-ro 3139beon-gil, Gangneung-si, Gangwondo	강원도 강릉시 율곡로 3139번길 24	Confucian yangban country estate residence—At least 500 years old. See page 165.	https://www.gn.go.kr/museum/index.do (in Korean) http://english.visitkorea.or.kr/enu/ATR/SI_EN_3_1_1_1.jsp?cid=264191
Sangwonsa Temple	상원사	1211-14 Odaesan-ro, Jinbu-myeon, Pyeongchang-gun, Gangwon-do, South Korea	강원도 평창군 진부면 오대산로 1211–14	Founded during Silla dynasty. Close to Woljeongsa temple.	
Seolleung & Jeongneung	선릉 · 정릉	1, Seolleung-ro 100-gil, Gangnam-gu, Seoul	서울특별시 강남구 선릉로100길 1	Royal Tomb Park—Final resting place of two Joseon dynasty monarchs. Easy to visit because it is close to Gangnam and COEX Mall in Seoul. See page 112. (Do not confuse with Jeongneung near Kookmin university.)	http://english.cha.go.kr/html/HtmlPage.do?pg=/royal/RoyalTombs_6_Seolleung.jsp&mn=EN_02_04 http://english.visitkorea.or.kr/enu/ATR/SI_EN_3_1_1_1.jsp?cid=264106
Seongyojang	선교장	63, Unjeong-gil, Gangneung-si, Gangwondo	강원도 강릉시 운정길 63	Confucian yangban country estate residence—Almost three hundred years old. See page 160.	http://www.knsgj.net (in Korean) http://english.visitkorea.or.kr/enu/ATR/SI_EN_3_1_1_1.jsp?cid=264372
Seoseokji	서석지	10, Seoseokji 1-gil, Ibam-myeon, Yeongyang-gun, Gyeongsangbukdo	경상북도 영양군 입암면 서석지1길 10	Confucian scholarly retreat garden—Small but perfect, built by a student of Toegye and influenced by Dosan Seowon garden but less austere. See page 178.	http://blog.naver.com/gbnadri/220824067597 (in Korean)
Songgwangsa Temple	송광사	100, Songgwangsaan-gil, Songgwang-myeon, Suncheon-si, Jeollanam-do, Republic of Korea	전라남도 순천시 송광면 송광사안길 100	One of the 'three jewels' of Korean Buddhism with a beautiful ritual walkway and rainbow bridge.	www.songgwangsa.org
Soswaewon	소쇄원	17, Soswaewon-gil, Nam-myeon, Damyang-gun, Jeollanamdo	전라남도 담양군 남면 소쇄원길 17	Most famous and most visited of the Confucian scholarly retreat gardens. More than 500 years old. See page 151.	http://www.soswaewon.co.kr (in Korean) http://english.visitkorea.or.kr/enu/ATR/SI_EN_3_1_1_1.jsp?cid=264336
Tongdosa Temple	통도사	108, Tongdosa-ro, Habuk-myeon, Yangsan-si, Gyeongsangnam-do, Republic of Korea	경상남도 양산시 하북면 통도사로 108	One of the 'three jewels' of Korean Buddhism founded in AD 643. Splendid ritual walkway with several stone bridges.	www.tongdosa.or.kr
Unmunsa Temple	운문사	264, Unmunsa-gil, Unmun-myeon, Cheongdo-gun, Gyeongsangbukdo	경상북도 청도군 운문면 운문사길 264	Buddhist temple garden—Surrounds the largest Buddhist nunnery in Korea. Almost one thousand five hundred years old. See page 134.	http://www.unmunsa.or.kr (in Korean) http://english.visitkorea.or.kr/enu/ATR/SI_EN_3_1_1_1.jsp?cid=806234
Woljeongsa Temple	월정사	374-8, Odaesan-ro, Jinbu-myeon, Pyeongchang-gun, Gangwon-do, South Korea	강원도 평창군 진부면 오대산로 374–8	Founded in AD 643. Home to numerous national treasures with a walking trail to its sister temple Sangwonsa.	woljeongsa.org
Wolji Pond	월지			See Donggung Palace and Wolji Pond.	
Yongho Garden	용호정원	29, Jinju-daero 1728beon-gil, Myeongseok-myeon, Jinju-si, Gyongsangnam-do	경상남도 진주시 명석면 진주대로 1728번길 29	Built in 1922 during Japanese occupation. Contains mounds representing Moutains of Wu. See pages 45-46, 48.	

Map of Korea Showing Location of Gardens

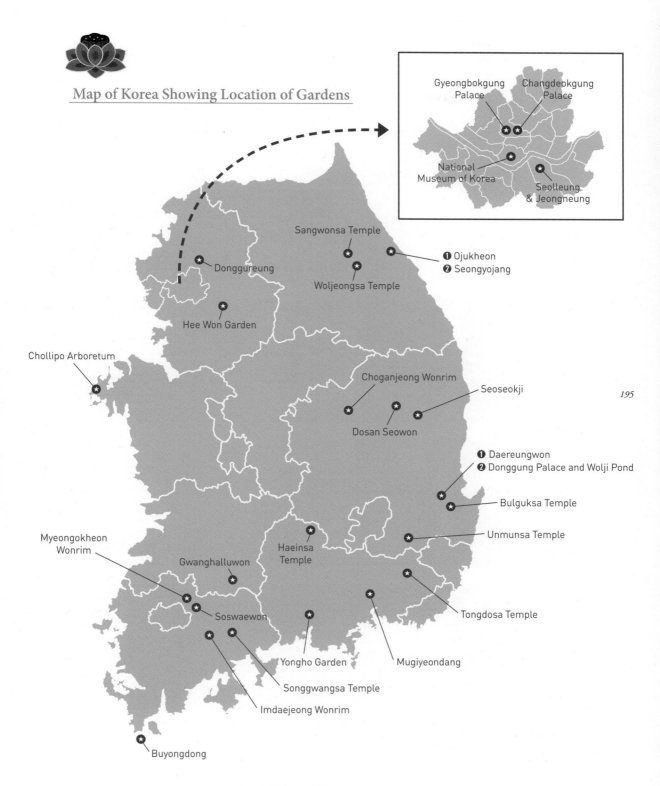

Gyeongbokgung Palace

Changdeokgung Palace

National Museum of Korea

Seolleung & Jeongneung

Sangwonsa Temple

❶ Ojukheon
❷ Seongyojang

Donggureung

Woljeongsa Temple

Hee Won Garden

Chollipo Arboretum

Choganjeong Wonrim

Seoseokji

Dosan Seowon

❶ Daereungwon
❷ Donggung Palace and Wolji Pond

Bulguksa Temple

Unmunsa Temple

Myeongokheon Wonrim

Haeinsa Temple

Gwanghalluwon

Tongdosa Temple

Soswaewon

Yongho Garden

Mugiyeondang

Songgwangsa Temple

Imdaejeong Wonrim

Buyongdong

195

Korean Dynasty List

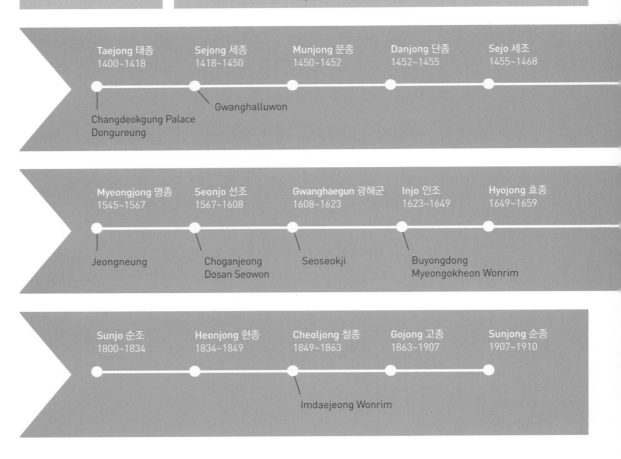

Gojoseon 고조선 2333 BC~108 BC	Goguryeo 고구려 37 BC~AD 668	Balhae 발해 698~926
	Baekje 백제 18 BC~AD 660	
	Silla 신라 57 BC~AD 935 Bulguksa Temple / Donggung Palace and Wolji Pond Daereungwon / Haeinsa Temple / Unmunsa Temple	

Taejong 태종 1400~1418 — Changdeokgung Palace / Dongureung
Sejong 세종 1418~1450 — Gwanghalluwon
Munjong 문종 1450~1452
Danjong 단종 1452~1455
Sejo 세조 1455~1468

Myeongjong 명종 1545~1567 — Jeongneung
Seonjo 선조 1567~1608 — Choganjeong / Dosan Seowon
Gwanghaegun 광해군 1608~1623 — Seoseokji
Injo 인조 1623~1649 — Buyongdong / Myeongokheon Wonrim
Hyojong 효종 1649~1659

Sunjo 순조 1800~1834
Heonjong 헌종 1834~1849
Cheoljong 철종 1849~1863 — Imdaejeong Wonrim
Gojong 고종 1863~1907
Sunjong 순종 1907~1910

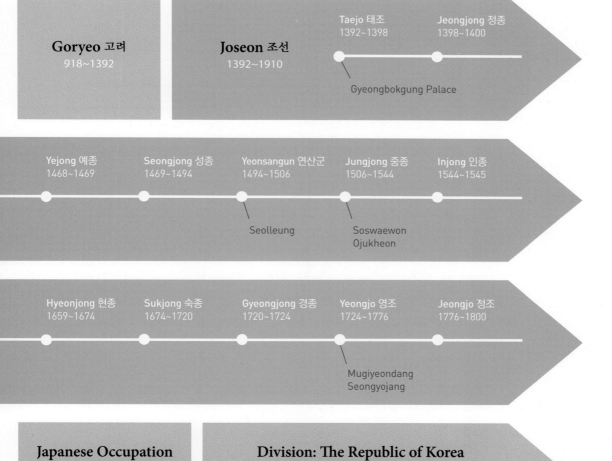

Goryeo 고려
918~1392

Joseon 조선
1392~1910

Taejo 태조
1392~1398

Jeongjong 정종
1398~1400

Gyeongbokgung Palace

Yejong 예종
1468~1469

Seongjong 성종
1469~1494

Yeonsangun 연산군
1494~1506

Jungjong 중종
1506~1544

Injong 인종
1544~1545

Seolleung

Soswaewon
Ojukheon

Hyeonjong 현종
1659~1674

Sukjong 숙종
1674~1720

Gyeongjong 경종
1720~1724

Yeongjo 영조
1724~1776

Jeongjo 정조
1776~1800

Mugiyeondang
Seongyojang

Japanese Occupation
일제강점기
1910~1945

Yongho Garden

Division: The Republic of Korea
대한민국
1945~

Chollipo Arboretum / Hee Won Garden
National Museum of Korea

197

Glossary of Korean Gardening Terms

Word	Hangeul (Chinese)	Meaning
-bukdo	북도 (北道)	Suffix meaning north province.
-dae	대 (臺)	A high platform made by piling flat stones. Also a suffix indicating such a place.
-do	도 (道, 島)	Suffix meaning province or island.
-gak	각 (閣)	Suffix meaning small stand-alone pavilion. Most commonly found at the back of Buddhist temples housing the shrine to *sanshin*, the shamanistic mountain deity.
-gang	강 (江)	Suffix meaning river.
-gun	군 (郡)	Suffix meaning county.
-gung	궁 (宮)	Suffix meaning palace.
-ji	지 (池)	Suffix meaning pond.
-mun	문 (門)	Suffix meaning gate.
-myeon	면 (面)	Suffix meaning town.
-myo	묘 (墓)	Suffix indicating the graves of noble men and commoners.
-namdo	남도 (南道)	Suffix meaning south province.
-neung or -reung	능, 릉 (陵)	Suffix indicating the grave of a king or queen.
-ri	리 (里)	Suffix meaning village.
-sa	사 (寺)	Suffix meaning temple.
-san	산 (山)	Suffix meaning mountain.
-won	원 (園)	Suffix indicating the graves of a prince, princess or important concubine. Alternate meaning, park.
Bongrae Bangjang Yeongju	봉래 (蓬萊) 방장 (方丈) 영주 (瀛州)	Three mythical mountains identical to Penglai, Fanzhang and Yingzhou in Chinese myth, thought to be the home of the immortals. Symbolic representations of these mountains occur in Korean gardens as three islands in ponds or occasionally as sets of three rocks either on shore or on islands.

byeotjip	볏짚	Form of greenhouse with walls made of rice straw for forcing out-of-season plants and blossoms.
cheonwangmun	천왕문 (天王門)	'Four heavenly kings gate,' the third of the symbolic gates on the ritual walkway leading to Buddhist temples.
chukgyeong	축경 (縮景)	Miniaturized landscape.
Daedong unbu gunok	대동운부군옥 (大東韻府群玉)	Encyclopedia of Korea Arranged by Rhyme. Details in description of Choganjeong Scholarly Retreat Garden.
daetdol	댓돌	External symbolic stone step designed to emphasise the passage from one realm to another e.g. from the women's quarters to the master's study in a *yangban* house or from garden to study hall in a *seowon*.
dancheong	단청 (丹靑)	Korean traditional decorative colouring on wooden buildings based on five basic colours each representing a direction: blue (east), white (west), red (south), black (north), and yellow (centre). Often appearing on palace and temple buildings depicting numerous botanical motifs, especially the parts of the lotus plant and the five white petals of the plum blossom.
dangsan namu	당산나무 (堂山木)	Holy tree in traditional villages, the centre of old rituals, believed to bring good fortune and weep at misfortune.
geumgangmun	금강문 (金剛門)	'Diamond gate,' the second of the symbolic gates on the ritual walkway leading to Buddhist temples.
gwageo	과거 (科擧)	All important civil service entrance exam operating for 900 years from AD 958, during Goryeo and Joseon dynasties. See also *yangban*.
gwana	관아 (官衙)	Provincial administrative complex including gardens.
hamaseok	하마석 (下馬石)	Dismounting stone in a garden. Originally this was where a guest tied his horse before walking through the garden to the house, temple, or palace. It is another symbol for transition from one realm to another.
hanji	한지 (韓紙)	Korean traditional paper handmade from the inner bark of the paper mulberry tree, a native of the mountainsides of Korea. It is extremely durable and was a valued export to China for many centuries. Today it is used in much paper craft including the creation of lotus lanterns to decorate Buddhist temples.
hwagye	화계 (花階)	Terraced flower-bed, usually planted with flowers and shrubs which clearly emphasise the passage of the four seasons.
iljumun	일주문 (一柱門)	'One-pillar gate,' the first of the symbolic gates on the ritual walkway leading to Buddhist temples.
jangdokdae	장독대	Outdoor terrace containing a series of glazed terracotta vessels for the storage of several fermented foods principally *kimchi*, a *kimchi* terrace.
jeong or *jeongja*	정 (亭), 정자 (亭子)	Pavilion—a place to rest and sit for a while especially in a spot where we can enjoy natural scenery.

jeongipum	정이품 (正二品)	A high courtly rank unusually conferred on a Korean red pine tree by King Sejo after he sheltered under it.
Jeongudang	정우당 (淨友塘)	Small pond for lotus. Like a clean friend the lotus is a pure flower despite having its roots in mud.
jongga	종가 (宗家)	Korean clan system in which the senior male member of each generation is responsible for maintaining the ancestral seat, and often, associated gardens. One of the main reasons so many private Korean gardens have survived for so long.
Neo-Confucianism	성리학 (性理學)	This strict form of Confucianism became the state ideology during the latter part of Joseon when several significant Neo-Confucian intellectuals built academies (*seowon*) with beautiful and influential gardens. Buddhism was discouraged and with it the much older Buddhist gardening tradition.
pungnyudo	풍류도 (風流道)	Ancient Korean religion which emphasised communing with nature particularly mountains and rivers in the search for enlightenment and immortality.
pungsu	풍수지리 (風水地理)	Korean equivalent of Chinese *fengshui*, traditional geomancy.
Samsinsan	삼신산 (三神山)	Three divine mountains, abodes of the immortals, often represented by stones or islands in Korean gardens.
sanshin	산신 (山神)	Mountain spirit often depicted in his or her own pavilion (*gak*) at the back of Buddhist temples, accompanied by tigers, pine trees and other symbols of immortality.
sagunja	사군자 (四君子)	1. Four Noble Friends—a symbolic set of plants commonly depicted in paintings and poetry and grown together in both Korean and Chinese gardens. They are: plum, orchid, chrysanthemum and bamboo. 2. Form of traditional Korean painting where the subject is the Four Noble Friends—plum, orchid, chrysanthemum and bamboo. Considered to be a form of meditation. Outdoors the orchid was sometimes replaced by pine.
Sehansamwu	세한삼우 (歲寒三友)	Three friends in winter—a symbolic set of plants commonly depicted in paintings and poetry and grown together in both Korean and Chinese gardens. They are: plum, pine tree and bamboo.
seokgasan	석가산 (石假山)	Artificial mountain.
Seon Buddhism (Seonjong)	선불교 (禪佛敎)	Syncretic Korean form of Buddhism which blends Chinese Zen and Pure land Buddhism, Daoism and earlier Korean spiritual beliefs such as belief in mountain spirits and the sacredness of mountains and the natural environment. Seon Buddhist monks developed *pungsu*, the unique system of geomancy so important for Korean garden design.
seonbi	선비	Moral rectitude and virtuous scholar. Often one who had given up preferment at court and retired to the country to study and build a beautiful garden.

seowon	서원(書院)	Privately founded Confucian academies.
sipjangsaeng	십장생(十長生)	The 10 Korean symbols of longevity: sun, mountains, water, clouds, rock, pine trees, mushrooms, white cranes, turtles and deer. Often found in palace and temple paintings and garden decorations, such as on the tiles in the Queen's garden in Gyeongbokgung Palace in Seoul.
sonamu	소나무	Korean red pine. Although not officially, this tree is widely regarded as the Korean national symbol and symbol for royalty and long life.
suseok	수석(壽石)	Symbolic arrangement of rocks, commonly three or nine.
Tripitaka Koreana	팔만대장경(八萬大藏經)	The world's most comprehensive and oldest intact version of Buddhist canon carved onto 81,258 wooden printing blocks in the 13th century. Housed in Haeinsa Temple.
ui-won	의원(意園)	An imaginary garden. A parlour game played by members of the Korean elite who designed gardens in their minds and then rendered them in paintings or poetry.
um-yang	음양(陰陽)	The Korean version of the Chinese idea of *yin-yang*, the balance achieved by opposites such as male/female, light/dark, and thus the essential complementarity of the universe. The *um-yang* symbol features on the Korean flag where it is referred to as the *taegeuk*.
wonrim	원림(園林)	Nature garden.
yangban	양반(兩班)	Korean aristocratic status achieved partly by meritocracy demonstrated by the all-important Civil Service Exam (*gwageo*) and partly by inheritance. By guaranteeing feudal lands and leisure and encouraging education and study for at least three generations, it allowed the creation and maintenance of many old family gardens.

Further Readings

· **Gardens of Korea: Harmony of Intellect and Nature**

Heo Kyun. Translated by Donald L. Baker. London: Saffron, 2005

A wonderful book which describes many existing traditional Korean gardens in detail. I have taken many of the ideas expressed in my book from this book and in some cases, such as my explanation of Gwon Mun-hae and his Encyclopedia for Writers, quoted directly.

· **Korean Gardens: The Beauty of Korean Gardens Represents a Spiritual World through Their Historical Development**

Min Kyung-hyun. Seoul: Borim, 1992

The earliest book in English, now out of print. A splendid informative description of Korean gardens of all types from pre-history to the end of Joseon period.

· **Korean Traditional Landscape Architecture**

The Korean Institute of Traditional Landscape Architecture. Carlsbad, CA and Seoul: Hollym, 2007

Chapters by 13 different Professors of Landscape Architecture and associated disciplines.

· **Traditional Korean Gardens: Representative Gardens of the Joseon Period**

Korean National Arboretum. Seoul: Advan Publishing Inc., 2012

Survey with maps and many beautiful photographs and identifications of representative plants and trees in 26 Joseon period gardens.

- **The Culture of Fengshui in Korea: An Exploration of East Asian Geomancy**

Yoon Hong-key. Plymouth: Lexington Books, 2006

Detailed, clear explanation of *fengshui* principles and their application to the siting of houses, graves, palaces, towns and cities especially Seoul, and the Japanese destruction of Seoul's *fengshui*.

- **Forests and Korean Culture**

Chun Young-woo. Translated by Yi Cheong-ho. Seoul: Bookshill, 2010

A passionate, idiosyncratic plea for the preservation and veneration of Korea's trees, forests and the recognition of their fundamental importance to Korean culture and its environment.

- **Visits to the Kings: Guidebook of Royal Tombs of the Joseon Dynasty**

Lee Byeong-yu. Seoul: Geomarketing Co., 2008

Excellent photos and maps of the major tombs in Seoul, which together comprise a UNESCO World Heritage Site. Indispensible for visitors, with practical details of transport, opening hours and dates of ceremonies, as well as history of the individuals buried in each tomb.

- **Royal Tombs of the Joseon Dynasty: Legacies of Elegance**

National Research Institute of Cultural Heritage. Seoul: Nulwa Publishing Co., 2007

Lavish photographic survey of 40 Joseon dynasty tombs in and around Seoul, with descriptions of each tomb and brief history of each royal occupant.

- **Stone, Walls and Paths**

  Yim Seock-jae. Seoul: Ewha Woman's University Press, 2005

  An erudite explanation of the cultural and religious symbolism of stonemasonry in Korean traditional places such as temples and palaces. Copiously illustrated in colour.

- **Seowon: The Architecture of Korea's Private Academies**

  Lee Sang-hae. Carlsbad, CA and Seoul: Hollym, 2005

  Copious colour photos of surviving *seowon* and location map. Explanation of politics of *seowon*. Only passing reference to their gardens however.

- **Palaces of Korea**

  Kim Dong-uk. Carlsbad, CA and Seoul: Hollym, 2006

  Colour photos of surviving and restored palaces with gardens included incidentally.

- **Temples of Korea**

  Yoo Myeong-jong. Seoul: Discovery Media Korea Foundation, 2009

  Photos and history of 17 major Buddhist temples in Korea.

- **Korea's Historic Clans: Family Traditions of the Jongga**

  Korea Essentials No. 19, Seoul Selection, 2014

Website

· **Cultural Heritage Administration of Korea**

http://english.cha.go.kr

· **Imagine Your Korea**

http://english.visitkorea.or.kr

The official Korean Government Tourism site. Lots of practical information about how to get to cultural sites and some brief histories.

· **KoreanLII**

http://www.koreanlii.or.kr

A site with many resources and articles about aspects of Korean society especially law but including scattered material concerning gardens and horticulture.

Photo Credits

The author acknowledges the great assistance of the Korean National Arboretum (KNA) and the Korean Tourist Organisation (KTO) in allowing the use of several of their photos in her book. While the majority of the photos are her own, there are also photos by Lily Matthews, Graham Greenleaf, Suh Jae-Sik and others. Each is acknowledged in the accompanying caption.

Index